Ivankovic

SCHOLASTIC

Parts of Speech

Made Fun

By Jim Halverson

New York ◆ Toronto ◆ London ◆ Auckland ◆ Sydney
Mexico City ◆ New Delhi ◆ Hong Kong ◆ Buenos Aires

Teaching
Resources

D1361189

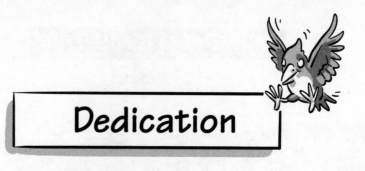

Dedication

With thanks to my students, my colleagues,
and, especially, my family.

Cover design by James Sarfati
Interior design by Grafica, Inc.
Interior illustrations by Dave Clegg

ISBN 0-439-51892-X

2 3 4 5 6 7 8 9 10   40   11 10 09 08 07 06 05 04

Table of Contents

Introduction

What This Book Is...

The exercises in this book rest upon two assumptions: that students learn best when they are having fun, and that most students need frequent repetition of grammatical concepts in order to retain them. These units are designed to help you address both needs. Instead of taking yet another grammar quiz to test and demonstrate their knowledge, students get to solve word puzzles, mazes, and mysteries.

The exercises are also designed to suit a range of teaching needs. They can be used by an entire class or for individual enrichment, and they reflect varying age and skill levels. Most units have three separate exercises, each a bit harder and more sophisticated than the one before it. (Some exercises address only part of a unit's concept—direct objects, for example, but not indirect objects.) You may find that only one of these is appropriate for the work you are doing or for the age level of your students, or you may wish to work your way through all of them.

...And Is Not

The introduction to each unit provides helpful definitions, rules, examples, and teaching tips. These introductions are not, however, designed to be complete teaching guides. Similarly, the exercises are meant to supplement your teaching, not to provide a complete or methodical program for each concept. For the easier parts of speech, the introduction to nouns, for instance, you may find that the exercises here are sufficient. But for difficult concepts, such as whether a word is being used as a preposition or an adverb, you are surely going to want to build up to the exercises with preliminary work. You can then use the mazes and games as enjoyable rewards for mastering the concepts.

Before You Start...

Since the exercises require that students have a working knowledge of the concepts involved, it is very important for you to familiarize yourself with a unit before using it. Make sure that you have covered all the grammatical issues that crop up. Within the unit, check the degrees of difficulty of the exercises and decide which pages best suit your students and your needs. Generally, the first page is probably best for fifth and sixth grades, the second for sixth and seventh grades, and the third for eighth and up, but these can be only very rough guidelines since classes and concepts vary so greatly. A few exercises, such as the one on subordinating conjunctions, are clearly meant only for students with a more sophisticated understanding of grammar.

...And After You Finish

I hope that you will connect the grammar activity pages in this book with real-world writing and help students see that an understanding of the parts of speech and the parts of a sentence is really just a small part of a bigger picture—written communication. The sooner they can make a grammatical concept "theirs" by applying it in their own writing, the sooner that concept will be theirs for life. For instance, after students work on exercises from the units on adjectives, you might give a writing assignment that asks them to use unusual adjectives in order to make a description vivid and fun. Or after doing exercises on prepositions and indefinite pronouns, you might have your students proofread their own writing for subject and verb agreement errors caused by intervening phrases—*One (of the boys) was there,* and not *One of the boys were there.*

Finally, don't forget that understanding sentence structure is just one of many English skills and not an end in itself. Some of your students—in fact, all of us at times—are going to continue to make grammatical errors, but such lapses should not prevent students from being appreciated as fine writers if their written communication is fresh, vivid, forceful, or delightful.

—Jim Halverson

Unit 1: Nouns

Focus

The exercises in this unit introduce students to the concept of parts of speech, showing them that finding nouns is a relatively easy task.

Grammar Tips

In many books nouns are defined as words that name a person, place, or thing. And, yes, the word noun is derived from the Latin word *nomen*, which means name. While the "person, place, or thing" definition is often adequate, it isn't always accurate, as the cartoon above illustrates. If you use the word *bird* to modify a noun—*bird brain*—then you have turned it into an adjective, a word that modifies a noun.

In English a word may have been born as a certain part of speech, but the moment it is used in a sentence in some other way, it becomes another part of speech. Is the word *book* a noun? Yes, very often. But, consider the use of **book** in these two sentences: *In my classroom I always have a* **book** *chart* (adjective) and *Before flying I* **book** *my flight* (verb).

Teaching Tips

There are several methods that help students spot nouns. The first is a variation on the "person, place, or thing" idea. Ask students to look for words that name or specify something, remembering that not all "things" are solid objects or living beings: *Laughter, sadness,* and *popularity* are abstract kinds of things.

A second test that often works is to insert *the* before the word in question—*the house, the nation.* If *the* (an adjective) fits, the word may be functioning as a noun. Caution: This method won't work well for proper nouns, like *Mary* or *Boston.* Also, you must be sure that the word is not being used as another part of speech that can also be a noun, such as the word *play* in *Let's play a game.* Note that in the second exercise there are a few cases of words usually used as nouns being used as adjectives.

Often a word's suffix is a tip-off that it is being used as a noun. Here is a short list of noun endings: *-tion, -ity, -ence, -ism, -ment, -ness.* Have students generate a more complete reference list of noun endings to post in the classroom.

Name _____   **Date** _____

Crack the Code

Directions: Circle the first letter of all the words used as nouns in these sentences. When you have found all of the nouns, the circled letters will form a short phrase, when taken in order from left to right. (You will have to separate the words that you make.)

Example: Cathy, who loves animals, lives in Texas. (cat)

1. I like most vegetables, but not eggplant.

2. The red roses in that yard are beautiful.

3. Does Gary really hate oatmeal?

4. The order for dinner was given to the waiter.

5. Olivia is a relative of the king.

Message: _____

Noun Find

Directions: Circle ten nouns in the sentences below. Then see if you can find them in the "noun find." They run up, down, across, and diagonally.

Bonus: Find one word in the "noun find" that is not a noun and yet can also be found in the sentences: _____

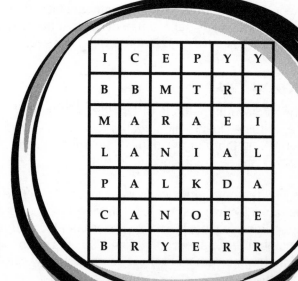

I	C	E	P	Y	Y
B	B	M	T	R	T
M	A	R	A	E	I
L	A	N	I	A	L
P	A	L	K	D	A
C	A	N	O	E	E
B	R	Y	E	R	R

1. As a reader he loved to escape from reality.

2. The bride was a very successful banker.

3. The damaged canoe had lain too long in the ice.

4. At the loud party the canary was happily singing too.

5. The lamp in the lane has gone out.

Parts of Speech Made Fun • Scholastic Teaching Resources

Name _____ **Date** _____

Help Maia

Help Maia decide whether she should climb the stone wall and take the shortcut across the field. She knows that the farmer who owns the field wouldn't care, unless his geese are out. (Geese can be very aggressive.) You can help Maia decide if it's all right to cross by doing the following exercise.

Directions: Circle all the words used as nouns in the following sentences. Then shade in the stones that correspond to the numbers over those nouns to reveal a message in the wall that will help Maia. *Hint:* Some words that are often used as nouns are not used that way in these sentences.

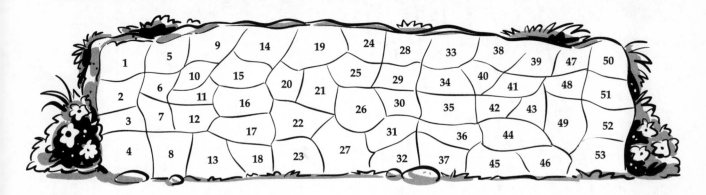

1.   20   26   3   52   33   46   15
   How did Henry heave that huge hippo to the top of his house?

2.   2   1   35 21   43   23   19
   The terrifying tiger tore a troublesome tear in her tutu.

3.   6   39   17   42   8   5   29   25   50
   When the price of plaster of Paris pushed up perilously, Paul plastered

      37   45   11   16
   his porch with plastic paste.

4.   9   49   34   4   22   36   48   14
   Seven silly sailors served salami sandwiches to the seasick soldiers.

5.   7   27   31 44   40   18   13   28   41
   Because the beauty of the bean bag beguiled Brenda, she bought it for her baby.

Maze

Directions: Find the correct path from the start (**S**) to the finish (**F**) by passing through 13 words in **boldface italics** that are being used as nouns. If the word is not being used as a noun, that area acts like a block and you must find another path. Be careful: there are false paths.

✳ **Bonus:** How many highlighted words are being used as nouns in the entire maze?

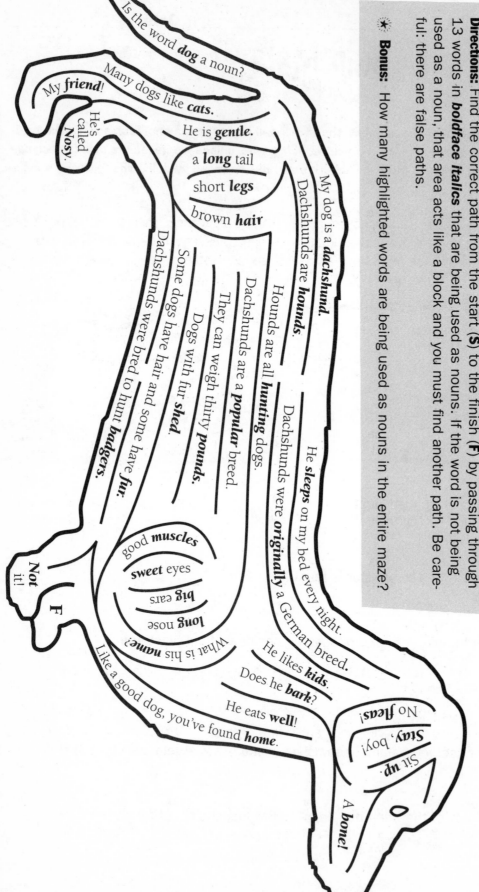

Is the word **dog** a noun?

Many dogs like **cats.**

My **friend**!

He is **gentle.**

He's called **Nosy.**

a **long** tail

short **legs**

brown **hair**

My dog is a **dachshund.**

Dachshunds are **hounds.**

Hounds are all **hunting** dogs.

Dachshunds are a **popular** breed.

They can weigh thirty **pounds.**

Dogs with fur **shed.**

Some dogs have hair and some have **fur.**

Dachshunds were bred to hunt **badgers.**

good **muscles**

sweet eyes

big ears

long nose

What is his **name?**

He **sleeps** on my bed every night.

Dachshunds were **originally** a German breed.

He likes **kids.**

Does he **bark**?

He eats **well**!

Like a good dog, you've found **home.**

Not it!

F

Sit up.

Stay, boy!

No **fleas**!

A **bone**!

Unit II: Adjectives

Adjective exercises are always the easiest ones in the grammar book.

I wonder if he knows that there are five adjectives in his sentence.

Focus

The exercises in this unit introduce adjectives. The more challenging second and third exercises require students to understand that words usually thought of as nouns become adjectives when they are used to modify a noun.

Grammar Tips

★ Why study adjectives (instead of pronouns) after nouns? By studying adjectives and nouns together, both parts of speech become easier for students to identify.

★ Many adjectives are easy to spot in front of the noun they modify—*red* dress, *large* number—but the abstract ones can be harder to identify: *that* dress, *any* number; the articles *a*, *an*, and *the*. And adjectives that follow the noun they modify can also be hard to recognize: The cat is *intelligent*.

★ Finally, any word can be turned into an adjective, no matter its usual use, if it is modifying a noun. The first bird in the cartoon above may not realize that he has turned the words *adjective* and *grammar*—words usually used as nouns—into adjectives in his sentence.

Teaching Tips

Adjectives literally modify our understanding of nouns by changing the way we perceive them. The noun *house*, for instance, becomes a much sharper image when we modify it with adjectives: **musty old** house. Let your students have fun with the concept of modifiers by putting a noun on the board—*house*, *car*, *animal*, *flower*—and invite them to modify it by supplying adjectives.

After students learn to spot the obvious adjectives placed right before nouns, introduce the more abstract ones, beginning with the articles and proceeding to words like *any*, *each*, and *another*, being careful to show them adjective, not pronoun, uses: **each** example (adjective), not **each** of *them* (pronoun).

Finally, be sure to teach a short lesson showing how words that are commonly used as nouns become adjectives when used to modify a noun: *garage* door, *spring* fever, *baseball* glove.

Name_____ Date _____

Hidden Message

Directions: Below are ten sentences that contain adjectives. Some of these adjectives have been underlined, *but many words that are not adjectives have also been underlined*. Circle only the underlined adjectives and then fit them into the answer grid so that the number of letters in each answer matches the number of spaces on the line exactly. The letters already in the grid will help you find the correct line for each adjective. When you are finished, the column of boxes will spell out a message. An example has been done for you.

1. The exercise seemed very easy?

2. My dog loves to get muddy.

3. The singer has a very low voice.

4. Marcia just saw a lovely yellow butterfly.

5. The actor was driving a new Italian car.

6. Our friends had such a pleasant time at the picnic.

7. Is Jane going to be helpful or troublesome?

8. The mashed potatoes made Jean feel full.

9. My grandfather has a tiny portable TV.

10. Was Karen eager to complete the message?

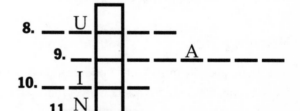

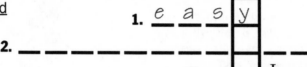

Parts of Speech Made Fun • Scholastic Teaching Resources

Guess the Numbers

Name_____ **Date** _____

There are 40 adjectives in the following sentences, and every one of them begins with one of six letters—*a, d, e, o, s,* or *t.* Take a few seconds to skim over the sentences and then make a guess about the number of times each letter begins an adjective. Put your guesses in the boxes next to the letter below. Then do the exercise to find the exact numbers. To help you, here are the numbers you should enter—but not in exactly the right order: 11, 8, 7, 6, 5, 3.

A ☐   D ☐   E ☐   O ☐   S ☐   T ☐

Directions: Check your guesses by underlining the adjectives and tallying the number of times each of the letters is used as the first letter of the adjective. Be careful. There are words in the sentences that are not used as adjectives but begin with *a, d, e, o, s,* or *t.* Don't count them.

1. We discovered a small pearl at the bottom of the old trunk.

2. The only time Patricia tried the orange drink she hated it.

3. Every one of these daisies has a short stem.

4. Sean recited dumb stories that he had learned at summer camp.

5. After a difficult day of organ concerts, he decided to take a short nap.

6. All children love those types of easy games.

7. That restaurant serves expensive but tasteless dishes.

8. Every one of these essays is successful and some are extraordinary.

9. We took an overgrown path to a special spot in the deep forest.

10. Sad Cindy hasn't any desire to read that ordinary diary.

Name_____ **Date** _____

Maze

Directions: Find your way from the start to the finish by passing through 17 areas containing words in **boldface italics** that are being used as adjectives. If the word is not being used as an adjective, that area acts as a block and you must find another path through.

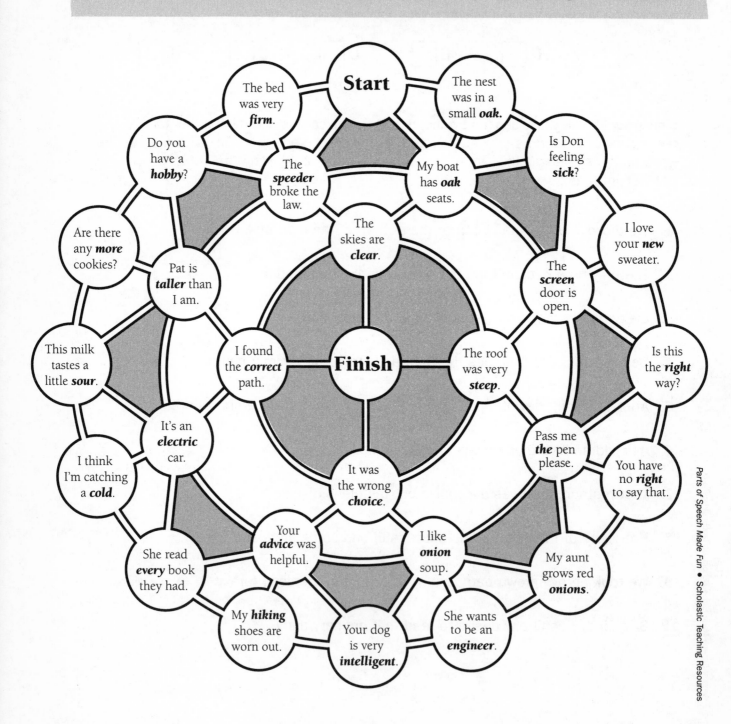

Parts of Speech Made Fun • Scholastic Teaching Resources

Unit III: Pronouns

Focus

Except for possessives, pronouns of every kind—personal, demonstrative, reflexive, indefinite, interrogative, and relative— are covered in the following exercises.

Grammar Tips

⭐ A word is a pronoun only if it's in a noun "slot" in a sentence—if it's a subject, object, predicate nominative, etc. This helps students when they have to deal with words like *that*, which can be used as a pronoun, adjective, or conjunction.

⭐ An important caution: When working with possessive pronouns (*his, our, its, mine* or any of the other possessive forms), notice how important it is to contrast adjective and pronoun usage—**his** book (possessive adjective) and **his** is broken (possessive pronoun).

Teaching Tips

To introduce pronouns, write on the board a sentence like this one: *Maria bought Maria and Maria's friend Susan tickets to a concert, and Maria and Susan both loved the concert.* Then ask if the style of that sentence seems awkward. Students will notice the repetitions, and together you and the class can improve the style by substituting pronouns for the repeated nouns: *Maria bought herself and her friend Susan tickets to a concert, and they both loved it.*

This method emphasizes that pronouns are used just like nouns, excepting the possessives, of course. (I explain possessives by pointing out that a noun in the possessive case—like *Maria's* above—is being used as an adjective.) This stress on use makes it much easier for me later to help students tell if words like *this, that, either,* and *some* are being used as pronouns or adjectives.

The following exercises become increasingly difficult as different types of pronouns are addressed: The first looks at personal (but not possessive), reflexive, demonstrative, and indefinite pronouns; the second covers all those of the first exercise plus the interrogative and relative pronouns. The maze, as always, reviews the entire unit. Note that the following exercises do not ask students to identify *his, our, its, mine* or any of the other possessives, as these should be taught in a lesson that contrasts adjective and pronoun usage (see the second pointer in grammar tips above).

Name_____ Date _____

Geography Puzzle

Question: How many states lie west of the Mississippi? Answer: _____

Directions: Circle all of the pronouns in the following sentences. In the space after each sentence, write the number of pronouns you circled. If you identify all the pronouns correctly, the numbers will add up to the number of states west of the Mississippi. (Do not count the example.) *Warning:* There are four types of pronouns in these sentences— *personal*, *reflexive*, *demonstrative*, and *indefinite*. Also, words often used as demonstrative or indefinite pronouns may be sometimes used here as adjectives, not as pronouns.

Example: I like that story about the time you flew an airplane.   2

1. After finding a ten dollar bill in the gutter, Sheila said to herself, "This is going to be a great day!"   _____

2. Everyone in the family likes that song except me.   _____

3. "Are all of you feeling proud of yourselves?" Mr. Thomas asked several of the students angrily.   _____

4. This book is one of Bobby's favorites.   _____

5. "A few of us thought you made up unfair problems," said Carla bravely, and the teacher himself agreed with her.   _____

6. In the past, most of the people made clothes for themselves.   _____

7. That is a very clean cat because she washes herself every day.   _____

8. Have any of you seen that comet in the evening sky?   _____

9. "This will be a mystifying moment!" exclaimed the magician, and then he asked if anyone in the audience wished to disappear.   _____

Parts of Speech Made Fun • Scholastic Teaching Resources

Coded Message

Name_____   **Date** _____

Directions: In the sentences below underline only the words with numbers over them that are being used as pronouns. Next, find the matching numbers in the answer grid and circle the letters under them. The letters you have circled spell out a message about your work. An example has been done for you. *Hint:* Sometimes *this, that* and similar words are being used as adjectives, not pronouns.

1	2	3	4	5	6	7	8	9	10	11	12	13	14	15
(Y)	A	L	O	U	S	T	H	U	A	P	S	V	E	A

16	17	18	19	20	21	22	23	24	25	26	27	28	29	30
C	T	I	M	O	R	N	M	C	A	L	E	N	T	D

31	32	33	34	35	36	37	38	39	40	41	42	43	44	45
A	R	T	J	H	W	T	H	E	N	I	T	W	L	Y

Message: ___Y_____

1. Do you know if somebody lives in that house that looks so scary?
   1   31   21   23   45   12

2. Bonkers is one of several funny characters in this book that I love.
   2   30   34   11   19   39 26

3. "Has anyone seen a pen like this?" asked Paulo, holding up one of Sal's.
      14   32   5   43   6   36

4. "Either of the two plans is acceptable to me," said the mayor, who was
   10   9   17   15   42   28   4

   smiling because she knew how good both of them were.
   41   27   3   18   8

5. Does anyone know what Mike's phone number is?" asked Wanda shyly.
   25   16   13   38   29

6. Neither teacher knows who that singer is.
   7   35   40 37

7. Dee said, "All of the reporters are asking what happened to this store."
   24   20   22   33   44

Name_____   Date _____

Maze

Directions: Find your way from the start to the finish by passing only through areas containing words in **boldface italics** that are being used as pronouns. If the word is not being used as a pronoun, that area acts as a block and you must find another path through. The correct path passes through 39 pronouns. **Warning:** This is a difficult maze. There are false paths that lead eventually to blocks, and all types of pronouns are included—personal, reflexive, demonstrative, relative, and indefinite. Also, words often used as pronouns may be used here as adjectives.

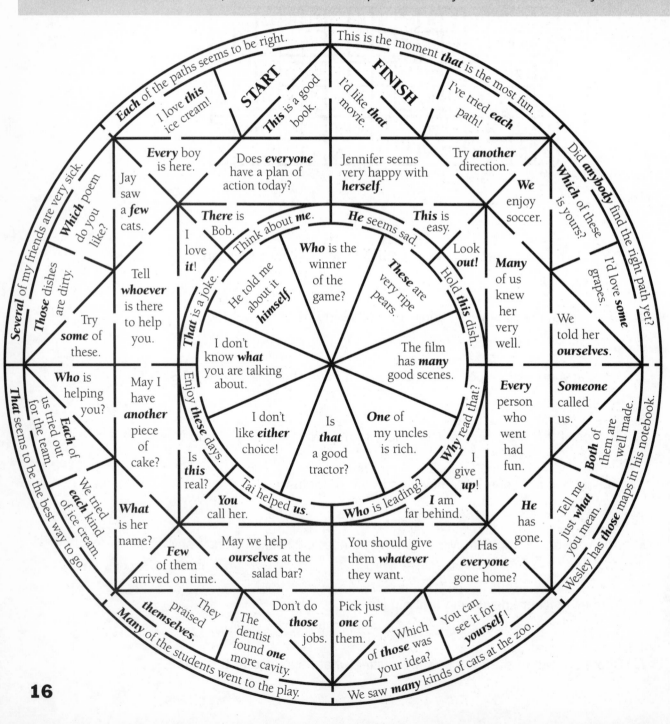

16

Unit IV: Noun, Pronoun, or Adjective?

Are there words that can be used as different parts of speech?

I'm about to say a word *that answers that question.*

Focus

This unit shows how the use of a word in a sentence determines its part of speech. The exercises here present the same word used in different ways, like *that* in the cartoon above, which is used first as a pronoun, then as an adjective.

Grammar Tips

★ The word *that* can be not only an adjective or a pronoun but also different types of pronouns—demonstrative and relative—well as a conjunction. The multiple usages of words like *that*, *some*, and *either* are often confusing to students.

★ Just as problematic for many students is the adjectival use of words that are listed in the dictionary as nouns—*In the **tree** (noun) is a **tree** (adjective) house.*

Teaching Tips

By concentrating on demonstrative adjectives and pronouns, you can help students get used to deferring judgment on a word's part of speech until they have fully analyzed its context. On the board write a few sentences that include *this*, *that*, *these*, and *those* used in both ways.

Example:

This tool should be held like *this*.
That is the picture taken by *that* friend of yours.

Once students feel comfortable with these four words, you can move on to samples of nouns used as adjectives—a *fly* swatter—and, for advanced groups, *that* used as a relative pronoun—the one *that* you like.

Note that the two exercises in this unit are fairly difficult and may not be appropriate for all students.

Name_____ Date _____

Skeleton Query

When we are newborns, we have over 300 bones in our bodies. Because some of these bones fuse, we actually have fewer than 300 by the time we are adults. How many bones do you think an adult has? Find out the answer to this question by identifying nouns, pronouns, and adjectives in the following sentences.

Answer:_____

Noun				
1	2	3	4	5
6	7	8	9	10
11	12	13	14	15
16	17	18	19	20
21	22	23	24	25
26	27	28	29	30
31	32	33	34	35

Pronoun				
1	2	3	4	5
6	7	8	9	10
11	12	13	14	15
16	17	18	19	20
21	22	23	24	25
26	27	28	29	30
31	32	33	34	35

Adjective				
1	2	3	4	5
6	7	8	9	10
11	12	13	14	15
16	17	18	19	20
21	22	23	24	25
26	27	28	29	30
31	32	33	34	35

Directions: Over the italicized words are numbers that correspond to the numbers in the three grids. Shade in a space that corresponds to the number over the word **but only** in the one grid that matches the way the word is being used—as a noun, a pronoun, or an adjective. When you have finished, the answer will appear in the grids. An example has been done for you.

1.   **3** pro.   **33**   **18**
   Is *that* the last *cookie* in *that* box?

2.   **4**   **16**   **34**   **30**   **21**
   Which cookie cutter did you use to make *those clay* ornaments?

3.   **20**   **33**   **7**   **19**
   Which of *these* is the best *clay* to use for making a *heavy* paperweight?

4.   **31**   **16**   **27**   **26**
   My *paper*, *which* was on the *porch*, looks like *that* because it rained.

5.   **30**   **4**   **3**   **3**
   Has *either* of you tasted *any* of *those* new ice cream *flavors*?

6.   **25** **2**   **10**   **23**
   "I don't like *either one*," said Laura, *who* was holding her *nose*.

7.   **21**   **33**   **35**   **34** **4** **6**
   One of my *homework assignments* is to find *some poems that* I like.

8.   **27**   **32**   **11** **32**
   This homework is easier than *some that* Mr. Forbes has given us.

9.   **10**   **15**   **25**
   In the *hospital* they put *ice* around the ankle *that* was sprained.

10. **34** **15**   **11**   **19**   **7** **22**
    Those who support *this candidate* hope he will defeat *all new* opponents.

Parts of Speech Made Fun • Scholastic Teaching Resources

Name_____ Date _____

Maze

Unit V: Verbs

Focus

The exercises in this unit let students practice finding verbs and also prepare them for finding complements by having them distinguish between action verbs and linking verbs.

Grammar Tips

★ It is essential that students be able to find the verb or verbs in a sentence. Indeed, finding the verb is the first thing that is usually taught when we parse a sentence. For students just getting acquainted with parts of speech, have them spot only action verbs in sentences that have no auxiliary (helping) verbs to complicate the process.

★ More often than not, English sentences contain auxiliary verbs that create longer verb phrases such as **have been** *wandering* or **might have** *gone*. Although these little words are very common, they are often overlooked.

★ Most English verbs are **action** verbs like *do*, *go*, and *think*, but our most common verb, *to be*, and a few others like *seem* and *become* are **linking** (also called **state of being**) verbs. It is crucial that students understand the distinction between the two because each type has a different set of complements—action verbs take direct and indirect objects; linking verbs yield predicate nominatives and predicate adjectives.

Teaching Tips

Students usually have little trouble spotting action verbs, and they quickly see that the regular verb endings—i.e., *-ed*, and *-ing*—can aid them. But common little verbs that often get overlooked or are misunderstood include the verbs *to be*, *to have*, and *to do* and auxiliary verbs like *can*, *should*, and *will*.

When students have a solid grasp of action verbs, introduce the concept of verb phrases, letting students see that in English a verb can be as many as four words long—*will have been running*. After working with auxiliary verbs, you may want to challenge students by using words like *have*, *do*, and *been* both as main verbs and as auxiliary verbs—*I have a pen* (main) and *I have been running* (auxiliary).

In this unit, the first exercise focuses on correct identification of action verbs only. The second exercise asks students to find all the verbs and to distinguish between main verbs and auxiliary verbs. The third exercise adds the problem of distinguishing the type of main verb—action or linking.

Parts of Speech Made Fun • Scholastic Teaching Resources

Name _____ **Date** _____

Riddle

What animal keeps the best time?

Answer: _____

Directions: Solve the riddle by finding the action verbs in the following sentences. First, underline each verb. After you have found the verbs, fit them into the answer grid. Be sure to use every space when entering a verb and to let the letters that are already entered guide you. An example has been done for you. **Hint:** There are no helping verbs, but two sentences have compound verbs (two or more verbs connected by *and*, *or*, or *but*).

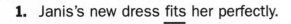

1. Janis's new dress <u>fits</u> her perfectly.

2. She tested the temperature of the baby's bath with her elbow.

3. Some riddles drive me crazy!

4. Draw a cat for me, Mikey.

5. The judge satisfied his demand and appointed a new lawyer.

6. This job requires a college degree and a year of training.

7. His father praised him for his good grades in school.

8. Water trickles into my basement after every big storm.

9. Becky brought her glove to the Red Sox game.

10. This field produces wonderful snow peas.

11. One hide-and-seek player crawled into the garage and hid in a garbage can.

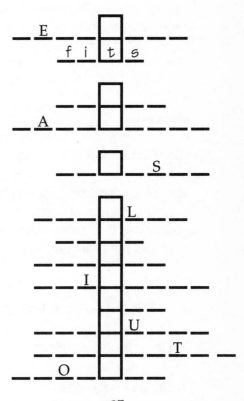

Main and auxiliary (helping)

Name _____ **Date** _____

Hidden Message

Serena is not really superstitious, but while absentmindedly brushing her hair this morning, the brush slipped and shattered her full-length mirror. It's her birthday today, and now she's worried that she'll get only disappointing presents. Find the name of her main present in her broken mirror and help Serena regain her serenity.

Directions: Many of the words in the sentences below are followed by a number-letter pair. These pairs refer to "fragments" of the mirror that you must shade in to reveal the hidden message. First, find and underline all the verbs. Then, decide if each verb underlined is a main verb or an auxiliary (helping) verb. If it's a main verb, then the letter (or double letter) after it tells you which fragment to shade in. If it's an auxiliary verb, then use the number as your guide. When you are done, Serena's main present will be clear. An example has been done for you.

aux.

1. Jody <u>will</u> **(14-f)** be **(54-aa)** giving **(26-k)** a party **(51-u)** this **(36-y)** weekend.

2. Don has **(40-dd)** been **(78-b)** asked **(29-11)** for **(62-q)** his advice **(9-oo)**.

3. Do **(19-i)** any **(82-jj)** of **(43-d)** you have **(33-p)** a birthday soon **(1-bb)**?

4. Someone **(44-s)** here **(24-uu)** should **(46-h)** have **(3-m)** known **(11-gg)** that **(71-z)** I was **(28-x)** going **(17-n)** out **(72-qq)** tonight.

5. Has **(21-g)** either **(49-pp)** of **(2-e)** them been **(34-r)** using **(5l-v)** my new pen?

6. When **(31-rr)** the storm finally **(66-o)** did **(75-ii)** reach **(8-cc)** us, we had **(65-u)** already **(25-t)** been **(32-ff)** in the cellar for **(10-y)** three hours.

7. If **(83-kk)** Bo had **(80-a)** been **(20-ss)** looking **(50-nn)**, he would **(58-q)** have **(39-ww)** seen **(12-mm)** the ball!

8. Could **(4-j)** Roberto have **(56-hh)** helped **(23-l)** me with **(6-i)** the chore?

9. What **(37-f)** have **(7-vv)** you been **(67-b)** doing **(18-w)** for so **(22-u)** long?

10. Kari **(37-x)** might **(48-e)** have **(42-tt)** been **(35-c)** asked, **(27-ee)** too.

Parts of Speech Made Fun • Scholastic Teaching Resources

Name_____ Date _____

Funny Fact

What action can we humans do easily that kangaroos can't do at all?

Answer: _____

Directions: To find the answer, identify and label all the verbs in the sentences below, according to their type. Under each verb write either *act.* for a main action verb, *aux.* for an auxiliary (helping) verb, or *link.* for a main linking verb. Next, match the number in the parentheses over the verb with a number in the corresponding grid and write the letter in the box below it. An example has been done for you. **Warning:** Not all words with letters and numbers over them are verbs.

Action							
1	2	3	4		5	6	7

Linking							
1	2	3		4	5	6	7

Auxiliary								
1	2	3	4	5	6	7	8	9
								S

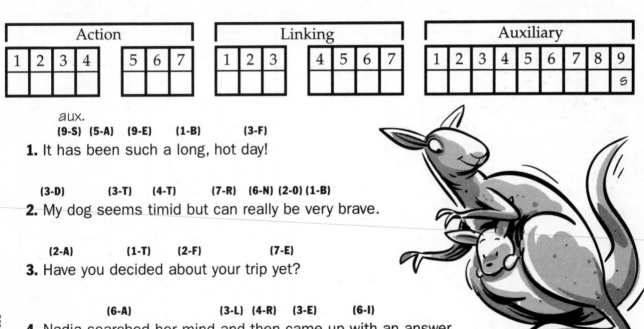

aux.
(9-S) (5-A) (9-E)   (1-B)   (3-F)
1. It has been such a long, hot day!

(3-D)   (3-T)   (4-T)   (7-R) (6-N) (2-0) (1-B)
2. My dog seems timid but can really be very brave.

(2-A)   (1-T) (2-F)   (7-E)
3. Have you decided about your trip yet?

(6-A)   (3-L) (4-R) (3-E)   (6-I)
4. Nadia searched her mind and then came up with an answer.

(6-A) (1-B) (6-L) (4-M) (3-V) (1-S) (8-D) (2-H)   (4-D)
5. He would have felt even worse if he had seen the accident.

(5-M)   (3-T) (4-Y)   (7E)   (1-N) (3-V)
6. Beyond the mountain pass lay a valley that looked safe to them.

(5-W) (4-T)   (7-N)   (3-L) (5-P)   (6-R)   (5-C)
7. Can either of you do this problem that my math teacher gave me?

(3-R) (7-K) (2-E) (6-H)   (4-K) (5-R) (3-C) (4-W)
8. The article was correct when it could easily have been wrong.

Name _____ **Date** _____

Double Maze

Directions: To reach the Action Verb Finish, follow only the sentences that contain action verbs. To reach the Linking Verb Finish, follow only the sentences that contain linking (state of being) verbs. The correct path to each finish passes through 23 sentences.

Bonus: There are four sentences with action verbs and four sentences with linking verbs that are not included in either path. Can you find them?

Start

I gave my dog a bath yesterday.

You should have been there!

Do you have any pets?

I've been here once.

You look tired.

How old are you?

Vicky cut her foot.

They have skim milk.

Think about it.

Are you sure?

Hold on tight!

It is hot today.

I love pears.

Do they sell pens in this store?

I have been sick.

They seem so unhappy!

The cake is done.

Do your math homework.

He should have been an actor.

The magician just disappeared!

Cross the street here.

Please be very still.

Was he helping?

That smells good!

She looks pretty.

I forgot my book.

Smell this mint.

He has been so quiet.

Feel this old satin.

It feels so soft!

Sound the alarm!

His voice sounds fine.

My dad was angry.

Try the new computer.

He was very careful.

He was making soup.

Everyone in the cave felt a little scared.

The teacher insisted on giving a quiz.

I have had a bad cold.

That hat looks silly.

Is she feeling cold?

Look at this!

The trip was really fun.

We are buying a new car.

This tastes sour.

Here it is!

He seems very smart.

Can you believe it?

I just found a dollar.

Don't drive too fast.

There has been a fire.

I wished for good luck.

Has he been away?

I need a haircut.

Action Verb Finish

Linking Verb Finish

Unit VI: Adverbs

Focus

The exercises in this unit introduce students to adverbs, beginning with easy –ly words like *clearly* and progressing to more difficult ones like *today*, *too*, and *therefore*.

Grammar Tips

⭐ It isn't always easy to identify adverbs because, as the cartoon illustrates, they certainly don't all end in -ly, and some are seemingly insignificant words, like *so* or *too*. Even harder for students to recognize are adverbs that can also be used as nouns—*today* and *tomorrow*—or prepositions—*fall **down** the stairs*.

⭐ The solution, as always, is to stress usage: if a word is modifying a verb, adjective, or other adverb, that makes it an adverb.

Example:

I have *always* liked you. (Adverb modifying verb *have liked*)
You have a *very* nice smile. (Adverb modifying adjective *nice*)
You flatter me *so* often. (Adverb modifying adverb *often*)

To check which word is being modified, read the word in question with other words in the sentence as a test. For instance, in the second example above, try, "Very have?" No. "Very smile?" No. "Very nice?" Yes, *very* modifies *nice*.

⭐ Adverbs often answer the questions *Where?* or *When?*—a fact that helps students with words like *today* or *there*.

Teaching Tips

To teach adverbs, you might begin with easy ones that end in -ly and clearly modify the verb in the sentence: *He ran **quickly***. Next, show that adverbs modifying the verb can often, unlike most other parts of speech, be moved around in the sentence for emphasis—***Finally**, we're here* or *We're **finally** here*. When students feel comfortable with the adverbs that stand out, introduce the harder ones—*too, so, very, now, today*—telling them they may have to work backwards (as demonstrated in the second grammar tip) once they determine which word is being modified.

Note that the exercises in this unit follow this instructional order and increase in difficulty.

Name _____ **Date** _____

Hidden Message

Tony's old television set is acting up again. He'd like to have it fixed, but his parents say the set isn't worth repairing unless it would cost less than $125. Help Tony learn just how much the repair costs by revealing the message hidden in the static on the screen.

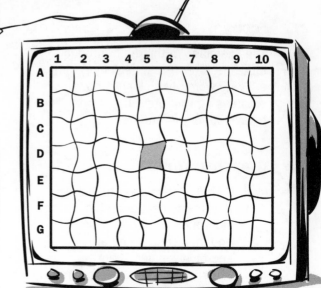

Directions: In the sentences below, if coordinates in parentheses follow an adverb, then darken the corresponding space on the TV screen. If the word is not an adverb, don't fill in that space. Ignore any adverbs that do not have coordinates following them. An example has been done for you.

adv

1. The bird **(3-C)** sang **(6-A)** happily **(5-D)** and loudly **(2-F)** in the old **(9-D)** tree, but

   suddenly **(10-D)** he chirped and **(4-A)** flew speedily **(5-B)** away.

2. Sadly **(10-B)**, I won't be arriving **(G-1)** early **(2-B)** enough to see **(7-D)** you.

3. Nina looked at **(5-E)** me angrily **(8-B)** and then said slowly **(4-B)**, "Unfortunately **(6-F)**,

   I feel **(1-C)** that **(6-C)** you should **(4-G)** go home immediately **(8-E)** before I get

   completely **(10-C)** upset."

4. Usually **(8-F)** we drive slowly **(2-D)**, but when my **(3-E)** brother broke his arm

   badly **(6-D)**, my mother really **(4-F)** rushed to **(10-A)** the hospital.

5. "I feel truly **(9-B)** sorry **(7-G)** for you," said the nurse sympathetically **(6-B)**, "but,

   unhappily **(5-F)**, I absolutely **(2-C)** must **(7-C)** give you this **(1-A)** shot."

6. "We'll arrive **(9-C)** eventually **(2-E)**," Mom said softly **(8-C)**. "Now you must **(3-F)** sit

   quietly **(8-D)** and patiently **(10-F)** and amuse **(8-A)** yourself **(3-D)** creatively **(9-F)**."

7. The peg supposedly **(10-E)** locked securely **(6-E)** in the slot, but **(5-C)** Cindy seemed

   totally **(4-D)** unable **(7-F)** to make it stay in permanently **(4-C)**.

Parts of Speech Made Fun • Scholastic Teaching Resources

Name_____ **Date** _____

What Year?

The words to "The Star Spangled Banner" were written in 1814 by Francis Scott Key, but it wasn't adopted by Congress as the national anthem of the United States until many years later. Guess what year the song became the official national anthem. Hint: It took more than one hundred years.

Answer: 19_____

Directions: To check your answer, find and underline all the adverbs in the following sentences. Write the total number of adverbs on the line above.

1. "Your kitten is so cute," said Estella enviously.

2. "I asked my mother again today if I could have one," she continued unhappily. "She, however, is very stubborn about it."

3. "Happily, you can always come here and play with Cotton," Brooke replied sympathetically.

4. "Sometimes my mom is almost an ogress! Yesterday I sneezed loudly and she made me vacuum my room," Estella pouted.

5. "Really, Estella," said Brooke diplomatically, "your mother must have a good reason for always refusing to get you a cat."

6. Estella moaned miserably, "She often says that I'm somewhat allergic to cats."

7. "I'm certainly not allergic!" Estella cried angrily. "I've been playing with your kitten now for an hour and... and... *achoo!*"

8. "I... I... *achoo!* I'll call you tomorrow," said Estella as she hurriedly prepared to leave.

9. Brooke then said sadly, "Your face is very red. Maybe your mother is right."

Name_____   Date _____

Maze

You've come to the mall only to find that the central fountain has overflowed and most entrances are closed. Shoppers are allowed to go in one door, however, as long as they move through stores, avoiding most of the walkways. See if you can "shop" your way through the maze.

Directions: Pass only through areas containing words in boldface italics that are used as adverbs. If the word is not being used as an adverb, that "store" acts as a block and you must find another way. The correct path from the main entrance (**S**) to the side door (**F**) exit passes through 16 stores.

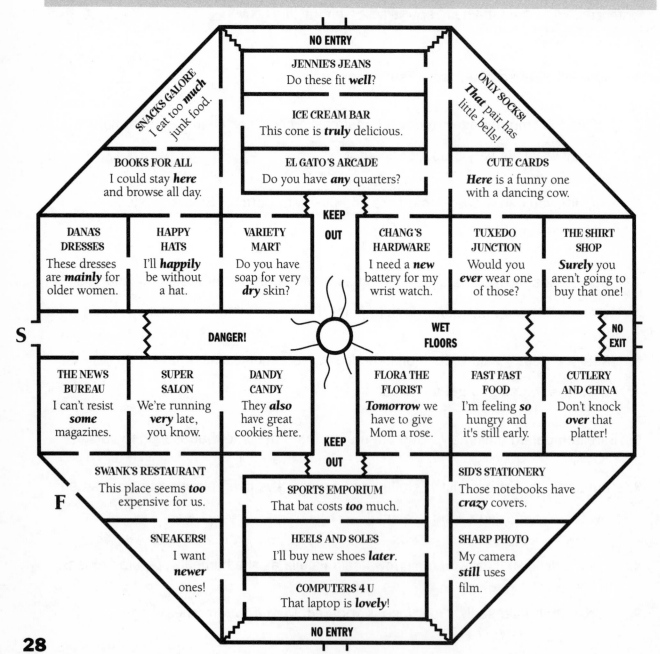

Unit VII: Prepositions and Prepositional Phrases

Focus

The exercises in this unit introduce prepositions and the harder ones challenge students to decide if words like *out* are being used as prepositions or adverbs.

Grammar Tips

- ★ A popular way to introduce prepositions is, as the first bird says, to say that they tell where a mouse can go—*over*, *around*, *through*, *into*, and so on—but this method quickly leads to difficulties. The word *of* is probably our most frequently used preposition: A mouse can go *of*?

- ★ Grammar book definitions often define prepositions as *words that connect nouns and pronouns to some other word in the sentence*. This is just as unhelpful since verbs can do the same thing. Compare *I cross the street* to *I walk across the street*.

- ★ A better way to help students think about prepositions is to call them connectives that begin a prepositional phrase. The stress, then, is on the whole phrase as a unit. This helps students distinguish between verbs and prepositions and, especially, between adverbs and prepositions, as in the difference between *He fell **down*** (adverb) and *He fell **down** the stairs* (preposition).

Teaching Tips

"Over the river and through the woods, to grandmother's house we go...." The first line of that old children's song makes a great introductory example of prepositions in context. Those three phrases in a row present a catchy example of the typical "shape" of a prepositional phrase—first the preposition, then modifiers, then a noun or pronoun object that answers the question "What?" that the preposition implicitly asks.

After putting a list of common prepositions on the board, ask students to make up their own phrases. Later, to differentiate between prepositions and adverbs, you might stress that prepositions must have objects, illustrating the point with sentences like *He walked **out*** (adverb) and *He walked **out** the door* (preposition).

Name_____ **Date** _____

Question & Answer

Question: In what year did all of the following occur: World War II began; a major league baseball game was on TV for the first time; the movie versions of *Gone With the Wind* and *The Wizard of Oz* opened.

Answer: 19_____

Directions: Underline the prepositions in the sentences below. Then write the number of prepositions in each sentence in the space provided. Write the total of these numbers in the answer space.

____ **1.** Across the street from Paula's house was a huge tree full of red apples.

____ **2.** From her bedroom window she could see the tree and the fence around it.

____ **3.** For several days she had been dreaming about those ripe apples.

____ **4.** The tree belonged to a man who never talked with his neighbors.

____ **5.** Aside from her father, no one on the block had ever spoken to him.

____ **6.** In a neighborly gesture, during a power failure, her father had once walked through deep snow and knocked on the man's door.

____ **7.** After a while the man had raised a window overhead and asked why he had come up his driveway.

____ **8.** After that rude reply, no one had ever gone beyond his property line.

____ **9.** Still, Paula could not help thinking now about slipping under his fence for just one of those red apples.

____ **10.** Against her better judgment, she even walked out the front door and along the road.

____ **11.** Should she cross the road and slip through the fence?

____ **12.** A kind of miracle saved her from trespassing and getting into trouble.

____ **13.** A gust of wind blew an apple off a high limb and over the fence towards her.

____ **14.** Paula darted after it and without a second thought bit into it and—oh, no! or maybe oh, good!—it tasted like a lemon!

Name_____ **Date** _____

Preposition Find

Directions: Eleven of the eighteen underlined words in these sentences are prepositions. Circle them and then confirm your answers by finding those words in the grid.

★ **Bonus:** Two words are used once as a preposition and once as an adverb. Write *adv.* over them when they are used as adverbs.

u	o	m	p	d	n	i	h	e	b	o
a	n	t	n	n	e	e	w	b	l	u
w	c	d	a	u	r	s	n	i	a	t
i	n	a	e	o	d	f	p	d	o	s
t	o	g	f	r	o	m	d	i	b	i
h	s	e	a	a	n	b	l	e	t	d
o	b	w	i	p	o	e	a	c	k	e
u	o	s	s	o	r	c	a	m	v	b
t	d	i	f	x	e	r	e	t	e	r
j	t	u	o	h	g	u	o	r	h	t

1. <u>Before</u> the game we are having a pep rally <u>outside</u> the stadium, but there are no events planned <u>afterwards</u>.

2. Gabby walked <u>inside</u> and saw a huge insect walking <u>towards</u> her.

3. <u>Underneath</u> the tree were presents <u>from</u> my relatives and <u>behind</u> it was a new bicycle.

4. <u>Despite</u> the fact that I had seen the movie <u>before</u>, I <u>still</u> enjoyed it.

5. <u>Throughout</u> the strange performance, the dancers stared <u>upwards</u> and moved <u>around</u> the stage awkwardly.

6. The coach yelled <u>across</u> the floor, "Don't just stand <u>around</u>! Even <u>without</u> the ball you must move!"

Name_____ Date _____

Maze

Directions: Find your way from the start (**S**) to the finish (**F**) by passing through 15 areas containing words in **boldface italics** that are used as prepositions. If the word is not being used as a preposition, that area acts as a block and you must find *another* path. The correct path to the finish passes through thirteen areas.

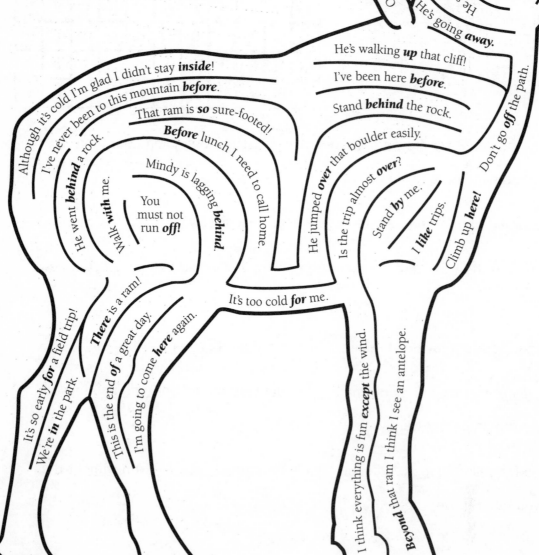
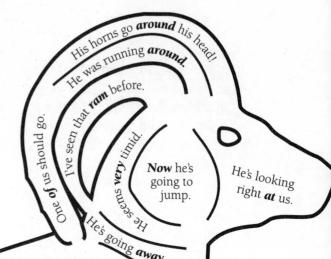

His horns go **around** his head!

He was running **around**.

I've seen that **ram** before.

One **of** us should go.

He seems **very** timid.

Now he's going to jump.

He's looking right **at** us.

He's going **away**.

He's walking **up** that cliff!

I've been here **before**.

Stand **behind** the rock.

Although it's cold I'm glad I didn't stay **inside**!

I've never been to this mountain **before**.

That ram is **so** sure-footed!

Before lunch I need to call home.

He went **behind** a rock.

Walk **with** me.

Mindy is lagging **behind**.

You must not run **off**!

He jumped **over** that boulder easily.

Is the trip almost **over**?

Stand **by** me.

I **like** trips.

Climb up **here**!

Don't go **off** the path.

It's too cold **for** me.

There is a ram!

This is the end **of** a great day.

I'm going to come **here** again.

It's so early **for** a field trip!

We're **in** the park.

I think everything is fun **except** the wind.

Beyond that ram I think I see an antelope.

S

F

32

Unit VIII: Conjunctions

Before is a subordinating conjunction.

Before saying that, you should remember that it can also be used in other ways—as a preposition, for instance.

Focus

The exercises in this unit let students practice identifying coordinating and subordinating conjunctions. Also included are words that can be used as subordinating conjunctions, adverbs, or prepositions.

Grammar Tips

★ Students have little difficulty identifying the coordinating conjunctions: *and, but, or, nor, for,* and *yet.* (Informally, we frequently use *so* as a conjunction meaning *therefore,* but since this usage is not considered good style, *so* is not included in these exercises.)

★ Subordinating conjunctions, which are used mainly to begin adverb clauses, cause more problems for students because many of them can also be used as adverbs or prepositions, like *when, where,* and *before.* It is crucial, therefore, to stress that subordinating conjunctions precede a clause, i.e., a group of words containing a subject and a verb—***When spring comes, we'll have a class picnic.***

Teaching Tips

Combine the study of conjunctions with short lessons on punctuation and style, letting students see a practical application of the study of parts of speech. With younger students, you might concentrate on the coordinating conjunctions and then work on the punctuation of items in a series and of main clauses joined by *and, but, yet,* and so on.

After going over subordinating conjunctions with older students, you might teach the punctuation of introductory adverb clauses and demonstrate their stylistic virtues. Compare *Because we are all tired, let's take a break* and *Let's take a break, for we are all tired.*

The first exercise asks students to find both types of conjunctions in simply constructed sentences. The second exercise and the maze challenge students to differentiate between words used sometimes as subordinating conjunctions and sometimes as other parts of speech.

Note: The correlative conjunctions—*either . . . or, both . . . and,* etc.—are not included in these exercises.

Parts of Speech Made Fun • Scholastic Teaching Resources

Name_____ **Date** _____

Puzzle

A man drove a black truck with broken lights around a turn. A woman in dark clothing was crossing the road in front of him. There were no lights of any kind—street lights, house lights, flashlights—and no moon or stars out. Still, they saw each other easily and an accident was avoided. How?

Answer: __ __   __ __ __   _a_   __ __ __ __ __   __ __ __.
           1 2   3 4 5   6   7 8 9 10 11   12 13 14

Directions: To find out the answer to the puzzle—or to check to see if you got it right—first circle the conjunctions in the sentences below. Then write the underlined letter over the corresponding number in the answer. An example has been done for you. **Hint:** There are both coordinating and subordinating conjunctions to find, and many words that are not being used as conjunctions have underlined letters.

1. After the storm there were branches (and) fallen trees in the road.
    2   12   6   4

2. Before we go, we should turn on one or two lights because it will
    9   7   13   11   5

be late when we return.
    3   1

3. Silvia and I won't call if you plan to sleep late after the party.
     4   1   10   12

4. Since we arrived yesterday, you have never stopped working.
    7   14   9

5. Although it may look funny, this hat is warm and practical.
    2   11   7   13

6. Until I met him, I thought that he was shorter than I am.
    8   8   5   14   10

7. During the test Naomi felt anxious and frightened, yet she was scoring very well.
   10   4   12   14   11

Subordinating conjunction, adverb, or preposition?

Question & Answer

Name_____ **Date** _____

Question: Wolfgang Amadeus Mozart was a musical prodigy whose talent became evident at an early age. At what age do you think he began to play the harpsichord? Answer: _____

Directions: To find the answer, or check if yours is correct, circle the words that are used as conjunctions in the sentences below. Then shade in the spaces in the grid that correspond to the coordinates under the conjunctions. Do not shade in spaces designated by words that are not conjunctions. An example has been done for you. **Hint:** Sometimes the same word may be used one time as a conjunction and another time as a different part of speech.

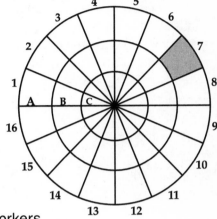

1. I'll come over (and) help you after lunch if you need extra workers.
B4   A7   A8   A12   C13

2. Since his mother got ill, Pierre has been very anxious, yet he still
B7   B14   C10   C4

manages to accomplish more than the rest of us do.
A9   B16 A14

3. You should get there before me because you have a better bicycle.
C8   B14   A5   C4

4. Does your mother or father ever complain when you play music?
A13   A15   A4

5. After we finish our game, I want to practice more, but I have to be
A3   B9   C1   C7

home by five because we're going to eat early.
A1   A6   B8

6. For everyone here there will be treats, for you have all done well.
C14   B12   A11   B15

7. As you know, we must work hard after lunch and finish this project.
A10   B1   A2   B10   C15

Name_____ Date _____

Maze

Directions: Find your way from the start (**S**) to the finish (**F**) by passing through 19 areas containing words in ***boldface italics*** that are used as conjunctions. (Both coordinating and subordinating conjunctions are included.) If the word is not being used as a conjunction, that area acts as a block and you must find another path.

★ **Bonus:** How many other areas that are *not* along the path contain conjunctions? ____

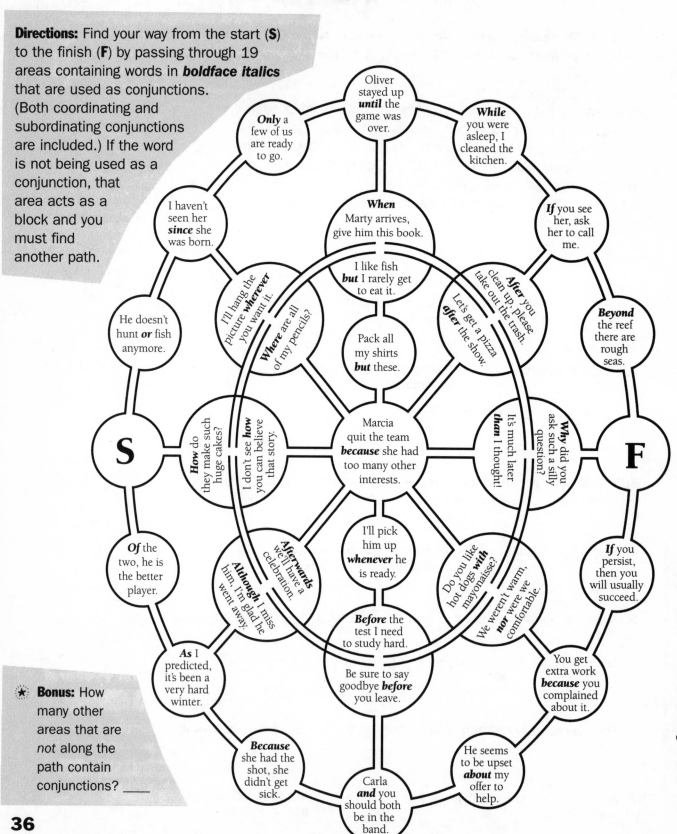

Oliver stayed up ***until*** the game was over.

Only a few of us are ready to go.

While you were asleep, I cleaned the kitchen.

When Marty arrives, give him this book.

If you see her, ask her to call me.

I haven't seen her ***since*** she was born.

I'll hang the picture ***wherever*** you want it.

Where are all of my pencils?

I like fish ***but*** I rarely get to eat it.

After you clean up, please take out the trash.

Let's get a pizza ***after*** the show.

He doesn't hunt ***or*** fish anymore.

Pack all my shirts ***but*** these.

Beyond the reef there are rough seas.

S

How do they make such huge cakes?

I don't see ***how*** you can believe that story.

Marcia quit the team ***because*** she had too many other interests.

It's much later ***than*** I thought!

Why did you ask such a silly question?

F

Of the two, he is the better player.

Afterwards we'll have a celebration.

Although I miss him, I'm glad he went away.

I'll pick him up ***whenever*** he is ready.

Do you like hot dogs ***with*** mayonaisse?

We weren't warm, ***nor*** were we comfortable.

If you persist, then you will usually succeed.

As I predicted, it's been a very hard winter.

Before the test I need to study hard.

Be sure to say goodbye ***before*** you leave.

You get extra work ***because*** you complained about it.

Because she had the shot, she didn't get sick.

Carla ***and*** you should both be in the band.

He seems to be upset ***about*** my offer to help.

Parts of Speech Made Fun • Scholastic Teaching Resources

36

Unit IX: Interjections

Hurray! Interjections are so easy—they express emotion and can never be used as another part of speech.

Now, now, my friend, you may now be saying something foolish.

Focus

This unit lets students practice finding interjections and presents them with the added challenge of recognizing when the same word is used as an interjection or another part of speech.

Grammar Tips

★ Although his reasoning is wrong, the first bird above is right about one thing: interjections *are* easy to spot and understand. They are words or expressions like *ouch*, *alas*, and *oh my!* that express emotion but have no grammatical relation to other words in the sentence.

★ Interjections are commonly used as the first word of a sentence—***Well***, *I'm not sure.* They can, however, interrupt ideas—*I think,* ***well***, *that maybe I'm wrong.*

★ Interjections can be misidentified if they are words, like *well*, that can be used as other parts of speech—*He sings* ***well*** (adv.).

Teaching Tips

The study of interjections offers a chance to have fun with grammar. After students understand their use and have spotted some interjections on their own, have them write some sentences in which they create unusual interjections from words that are not usually used that way, such as *rats!* and a few other unusual ones, such as *slime*, *fog*, and *grease*. Make sure that their sentences define the emotion that the interjection communicates,—*Oh, fog! I can't think today!*—and be sure that their choices are not just substitute or thinly veiled curses.

More often than not, interjections jump right out at students because they are the first words in the sentence and are set off with a comma or exclamation point. Since they cause students so few problems, this unit is comprised of only one maze. One note of caution: To make that maze a little more challenging and to emphasize the key idea that words may act as different parts of speech depending on their use, many of the interjections—like *now*, *well*, and *goodness*—are used as other parts of speech as well.

Name_____ Date _____

Maze

Directions: Find your way from the start (**S**) to the finish (**F**) by passing through 20 areas that contain a word or words used as interjections. If a sentence contains no interjections, that area acts as a block and you must find another path.

Hint: Some words used as an interjection in one area may be used as another part of speech in a nearby area.

S

Oh, no, this is not going to be easy.

Well, I think that this may be the right way.

Rats! I think I've taken the wrong path.

Wow! this is much easier than I expected.

Rats are rarely found in the mazes that I do.

Now, now, you must not get overconfident.

Yes, indeed, all of your friends wish you well.

I think now that I may have spoken too soon.

Hmm, are you sure about this decision?

Great! I feel as if I can do no wrong!

Oh, dear, I feel very unsure of this path.

That great feeling of mine didn't last long.

Bravo! We're doing well!

My dear friend just gave me a dirty look!

My, what a strange thought I just had.

Well, I've stayed right on track so far.

So, just what do you think you're doing?

I'm so very happy to be working with you.

Hey, I think that the teacher is sleeping!

Darn, I'm only half done now.

Yo, my friend, you're a very clever fellow.

Goodness! What are you saying to me?

Oh, I didn't know that you were sick.

Goodness and badness are not the subjects.

My darn old pencil keeps breaking.

What! You can't be serious about that!

Boo! I just caught you daydreaming.

Behold, the end of the maze is in sight.

Alas, we've just about reached the finish.

When I behold the end I get very happy.

There! I think that we have really done it.

There aren't any more choices for us to make.

Hooray! I do know my interjections!

F

★ **Bonus:** How many areas in the maze (both on and off the path) contain words used as interjections?

Unit X: Mixed Parts of Speech

Focus

The exercises in this unit review the parts of speech, stressing the importance of context in determining how a word is being used.

Grammar Tips

☀ The second bird recognizes that the word *well* can be several parts of speech, depending on its use in a sentence. He uses *well* once as an interjection and once as an adverb, but it can also be an adjective (*I feel well*), a noun (*The well is dry*), and a verb (*Tears well up*).

Teaching Tips

This unit can serve as a final review of the process of finding parts of speech or as a way to emphasize the importance of checking a word's context before deciding its part of speech. Do look the exercises over to make sure they offer an appropriate challenge for your students: the first one is much easier than the maze.

Prepare students for the exercises by writing playful sentences that use the same word in two or three different ways. Words like *well*, *that*, and *right* can each be used as three or more parts of speech, and students usually love to play detective, sorting out their usage.

Examples:

That (pronoun) reminds me *that* (conjunction) I am late for *that* (adjective) dentist appointment *that* (pronoun) I made yesterday.

I have a *right* (noun) to use my *right* (adjective) hand to *right* (verb) that little boat.

At the *ball* (adjective) game the umpire *balled* (verb) up the line-up sheet before throwing out the first *ball* (noun).

Same word, different parts of speech

Name_____ Date _____

Riddle

The short version of this story opening means the same thing as the long one. Can you figure out what the short version is?

VERSION ONE (long-winded):

A friendly, casual man, whose name is a nickname for Henry, approaches a woman, whose name is the English form of Maria, and greets her.

VERSION TWO (concise):

" _ _ _ _ _ , _ _ _ _ ," says _ E _ _ _ _ _ _ _ _ _.
  1 2 3 4 5 1 2 3 4   1 2 3 4 5 6 1 2 3 4 5
    Nouns   **Pronouns**   **Adjectives**   **Verbs**

Directions: To solve the riddle, or to check your solution, first write the part of speech of each underlined word—noun, pronoun, adjective, or verb—underneath the word in the sentences below. Then write the corresponding letter in the space indicated by the number-letter pair found above the word. *Be sure to write the letter in the area of the answer grid that matches the part of speech.* An example has been done for you. **Hint:** The letters over two words will not fit in at all because there are no spaces for them.

       2-E   5-Y   2-A   2-E

1. The <u>side</u> door was <u>left</u> open, and <u>that</u> is why the <u>duck</u> got out.
      adj.

            5-O   4-L   2-A

2. "Catch the ball with your <u>right</u> <u>hand</u>, and don't <u>duck</u>," said Mai.

    1-H   3-L 6-S   1-H

3. "<u>Hand</u> me <u>that</u> <u>note</u>," said the teacher, who had the <u>right</u> to demand it.

     3-R   6-L 5-O   4-L   4-R

4. "After <u>that</u>, I <u>need</u> a <u>rest</u>," said Dad after our <u>flat</u> tire. "<u>Watch</u> out

       6-W

for a <u>rest</u> area."

    1-M   3-R   4-Y

5. <u>Neither</u> of you can <u>rest</u> until you do <u>all</u> of the math, but the

   3-L   1-M

<u>rest</u> of <u>those</u> problems are easy.

Name _____

Date _____

Maze

Directions: Find your way from the start to the finish by passing through 14 boxes. You may enter any doorway (do not worry about the part of speech indicated in a doorway you enter), but to leave a box, you must use the doorway containing the part of speech of the word in **boldface.**

Hint: Some words are used as more than one part of speech.

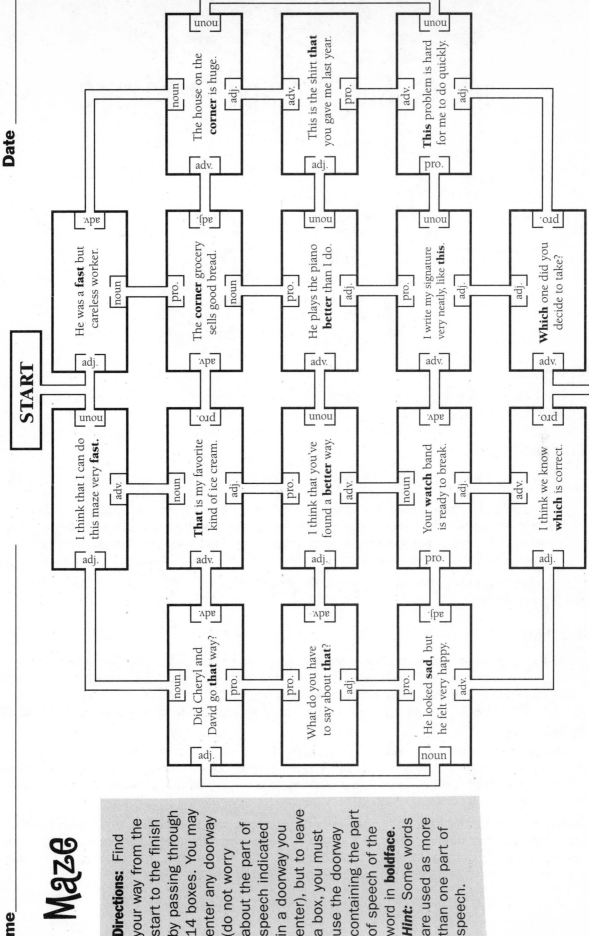

START

FINISH

Parts of Speech Made Fun • Scholastic Teaching Resources

Unit XI: Subject and Predicate

Focus

This unit introduces students to the concept of sentence parts with easy exercises in finding subjects and predicates.

Grammar Tips

★ Without an understanding of the essentials of an English sentence—the simple subject and simple predicate*—students can never hope to understand difficult formations such as noun clauses and verbal phrases. Nor can they avoid style problems like sentence fragments and run-on sentences when they write. The exercises in this unit are thus quite easy, designed to instill confidence by giving students immediate success, in hopes that this positive first impression will carry over when they encounter more complex grammatical concepts.

*For purposes of brevity, the simple subject and simple predicate will hereafter be called "the subject and verb."

Teaching Tips

Begin the study of sentence parts by writing a two-word sentence on the board—*Tom jumped*. Then show how one part of the sentence identifies the actor—the *subject* of the action—and the other expresses the action—the *predicate*. Next you might add phrases and modifiers—*Without looking, Tom jumped off the swing*. Point out that the main parts, subject and verb, have stayed the same.

Finally, you might teach the standard technique for finding subjects and verbs: First find the verb, then say *Who?* or *What?* before the verb to find the subject. This has to be refined later, of course, when intervening phrases come up—*One of the boys jumped*—but at first I keep it as simple as possible until the process is ingrained.

Notice that the first exercise has no compound subjects or compound verbs, and only in three instances are there auxiliary verbs. In the second exercise and the maze, compounds have been added, as have questions. More sophisticated problems—intervening phrases, subjects following the verb, imperative sentences, and so on—are covered in Unit XII.

Parts of Speech Made Fun • Scholastic Teaching Resources

Name_____ **Date** _____

Word Find

Directions: Find the simple subjects and simple predicates (the subjects and verbs) in the following sentences. Then check your answers in the word find. The subjects all run up, down, left, or right; the verbs run diagonally in all four possible directions. *Hint:* Three sentences contain auxiliary (helping) verbs and are included in the word find without a space—*willbe* for *will be,* for example.

l	s	p	a	c	k	a	g	e	g	y
a	a	t	d	d	l	e	r	n	u	h
w	i	u	o	u	e	e	i	x	n	t
i	l	a	g	h	w	v	a	d	c	o
f	b	c	s	h	a	m	i	n	l	r
e	o	e	a	h	e	s	l	r	e	o
l	a	w	e	n	e	d	b	c	r	d
l	t	r	s	i	w	c	a	e	v	a
o	e	i	l	d	r	i	b	t	e	r
w	t	f	f	r	i	e	n	d	s	n

1. The package arrived here yesterday.
2. That bird flies so beautifully.
3. After her party Dorothy cleaned the kitchen well.
4. The four friends were having a weekend sleepover.
5. Two huge dogs were in the doorway.
6. Your uncle has been here for an hour.
7. The old fellow with the funny moustache laughed at us.
8. The blue sailboat can win easily.

Compound subjects and verbs

Name_____ **Date** _____

Historical Question

Question: When he was inaugurated in 1961, John F. Kennedy was the youngest person ever to be elected president. How old do you think he was at that time? Answer: _____

Directions: To check your answer, first underline all the subjects and all the verbs in the sentences. Then add up the number of words you have underlined. The total number of underlined words is the answer to the question. **Hint:** For this exercise count every verb in a verb phrase—*has been running* counts as three verbs, not just one verb phrase.

Example: The old <u>dog</u> and young <u>cat</u> <u>are</u> <u>playing</u>. (Total=4. Don't count *old*, *young*, or *and*.)

1. The Svensons and Andersons have located many relatives in Sweden.

2. On Saturday my best friend and I are going to the beach and are entering the

volleyball tournament.

3. Did Paco or Frieda have the best grade on the science test?

4. You and your dog have so much in common and have had so much fun together.

5. Why are the desks and chairs in this new arrangement?

6. My mother and father sent in their coupons and received free baseball tickets.

7. Are you or your sister planning any outings this week?

8. Who dropped this paper on the rug and then just left it there?

9. Paula and her father have been working on the jigsaw puzzle for three weeks.

10. Who or what has opened my lunch bag and eaten my sandwich?

Review

Name _____

Date _____

Maze

Directions: Find your way from the start (**S**) in the mink's tail to the finish (**F**) in its nose by passing through 20 areas containing sentences with subjects and verbs indicated correctly—subjects in **boldface** and verbs in **boldface italics**. If any part of a verb phrase or one element of a compound subject or compound verb is not in the correct typeface, that area acts as a block and you must find another path. "**You** and I *ate*" and then left" would be a block because "I" and "left" are not in the correct typeface.

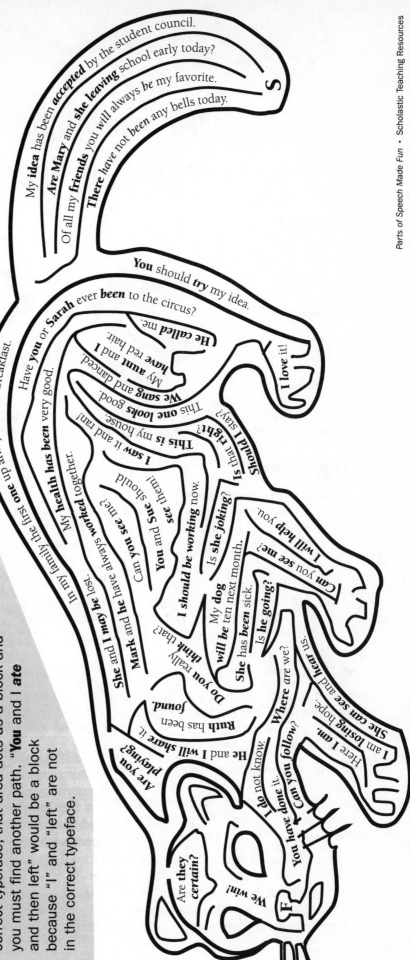

Unit XII: Subject and Predicate Problems

Finding subjects is so easy. They sit there right in front of the verb.

Watch out! There are other possibilities.

Focus

This unit deals with the "other possibilities" mentioned by the second bird, the constructions that often cause student problems when identifying the subject of a sentence.

Grammar Tips

★ Two tricky constructions are highlighted in the second bird's answer: imperative sentences in which the subject is implied but not stated (the *you* is understood) and sentences in which the subject follows the verb, such as sentences beginning with *here*, *there*, or *where*—*There are those birds* (subject: *birds*, verb: *are*).

★ Other more complicated constructions include sentences in which phrases come between the subject and verb, especially phrases following indefinite pronouns like *each*, *anyone*, and *all*—*All of the students were cheering.* (subject: *all*, verb: *were cheering*). Another complicating factor is the presence of verb phrases that include auxiliary verbs and compound subjects and verbs, the harder aspects of Unit XI.

Teaching Tips

With tricky constructions, take a different approach from the usual first step of teaching the basics of subject and predicate: Instead of having students first find the verb, ask students to work with prepositional phrases, so that they can mentally—or literally—cross out all the prepositional phrases before searching for the main parts of the sentence.

This approach saves many an error with sentences such as this: *Most of the students saw all of the game.* How many people would incorrectly say that *students,* rather than *Most,* is the subject of that sentence and *game* the direct object? This method also allows you to apply this grammar work to usage problems. After studying subjects and verbs, students can tackle agreement issues, such as *Each of the boys is* (not *are*) *here.*

The first exercise in this unit asks students to identify the subjects of imperative sentences and sentences in which the subject follows the verb. The second exercise and the maze cover questions and statements in which phrases come between the subject and verb, especially phrases following indefinite pronouns like *each*, *anyone*, and *all*. They also review verb phrases that include auxiliary verbs and compound subjects and verbs.

Parts of Speech Made Fun • Scholastic Teaching Resources

Imperative sentences and subjects that follow verbs

Name_____ Date _____

Hidden Message

Sheldon Sharky is an aspiring rock star. He's got his band, his unusual clothes, and his own song that he's sure will be a hit. It's called "I'd Even Eat Lima Beans for You." What *do* you think? Will it be a hit—or not? Shade in the spaces in Sheldon's shirt to learn the fate of Sheldon's song.

Directions: Underline and label (with an *s*) all of the subjects and (with a *v*) all of the verbs, including auxiliary verbs, in the following sentences. Notice that each sentence is followed by the word *you* in brackets in case the sentence is a command and the subject is an implied *you*. Then shade in the spaces in the shirt that correspond to the numbers following each subject or verb. An example has been done for you. **Hint:** Some numbered words are not verbs or subjects.

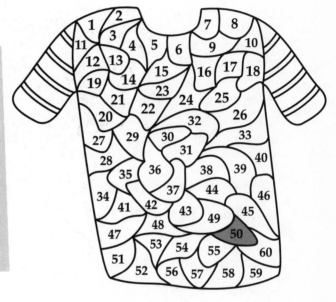

                                                v
1. Tell **(50)** Kim **(1)** about the spill **(58)** and ask **(3)** her for a rag. [you] **(30)**

2. Where **(25)** are **(14)** you **(43)** and Jan **(6)** going **(31)** after the game **(35)**? [you] **(53)**

3. In the pond **(39)** there were **(56)** three frogs **(22)** and a carp **(49)**. [you] **(20)**

4. Close **(37)** your eyes **(33)** and make **(60)** a wish **(54)** for good luck **(24)**. [you] **(57)**

5. After school **(5)** call **(36)** and tell **(23)** me **(17)** his **(29)** answer **(4)**. [you] **(13)**

6. There **(26)** should **(2)** be **(55)** more cookies **(12)** in this jar **(27)**! [you] **(7)**

7. When **(38)** are **(42)** Tai **(19)** and he **(32)** taking **(15)** the test **(21)**? [you] **(11)**

Name_____ **Date** _____

What's It Worth?

Our country is over two hundred years old, and in that time the dollar has changed in value because of inflation. Things that cost a dollar today used to cost only a fraction of a dollar in 1800. Of course, people were not richer then because they were also paid a fraction of what they are paid now. Imagine that you had $5 in 1800. Guess what it would be worth now.

Directions: To check your answer, underline and label all the subjects (s) and verbs (v) in the sentences below. Then add up the numbers after the words and write the total at the end of each sentence. Include all parts of a compound subject or verb and all auxiliary (helping) verbs. Notice that each sentence is followed by the word *you* in brackets in case the sentence is a command and the subject is an implied *you*. Add up those eight sub-totals to find what $5 in 1800 would be worth today. **Hint:** Many words with numbers following them are not being used as subjects or verbs.

1. Raul **(2)** and his **(1)** family **(3)** wanted **(4)** a change **(2)** and took **(3)** a trip **(4)** to Costa Rica **(1)**. [you] **(3)** ___

2. Can **(2)** you **(1)** really have **(3)** read **(2)** all **(4)** of those **(3)** books **(2)** in just one **(1)** day **(2)**? [you] **(3)** ___

3. Is **(2)** either **(3)** of your **(1)** dogs **(4)** trained **(2)** for hunting **(3)**? [you] **(3)** ___

4. Think **(4)** about my **(2)** idea **(3)** and give **(1)** me **(2)** an answer **(3)** soon **(4)**. [you] **(3)** ___

5. Why are **(2)** all **(1)** of you **(2)** laughing **(3)** and shouting **(4)** like that **(1)**? [you] **(3)** ___

6. There **(3)** have **(4)** been **(2)** thunderstorms **(3)** and hail **(1)** in our **(2)** area **(4)**. [you] **(3)** ___

7. Change **(1)** the oil **(4)** and give **(3)** the engine **(2)** a tune-up **(2)**, please. [you] **(3)** ___

8. Would **(3)** either **(2)** of you **(4)** like **(3)** another **(2)** helping **(1)** of turnips **(4)**? [you] **(3)** ___

Total: $5 in 1800 would now be worth about $_____.

Parts of Speech Made Fun • Scholastic Teaching Resources

Review

Maze

Subject and Predicate Problems

Directions: Find the path to the finish by passing only through areas where the subjects (including all parts of compounds) and the verbs (including all parts of compounds and all auxiliary verbs) are correctly identified. Subjects are shown by **boldface type**; verbs by **boldface italics**. If an area includes an incorrectly identified subject or verb or one that has not been highlighted in one of the boldface fonts, then that area is a block and you must find another path. The correct path goes through 11 areas not including the finish.

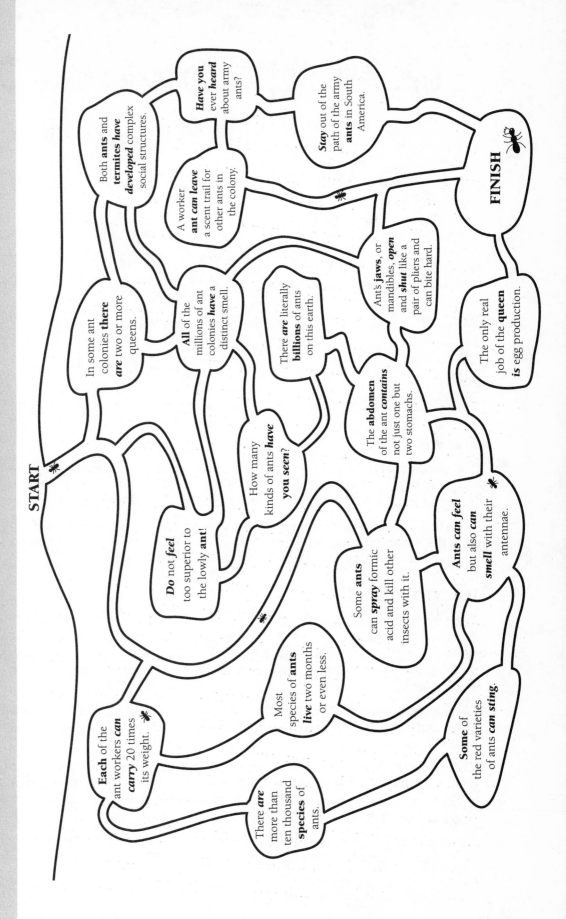

START

Do not *feel* too superior to the lowly **ant**!

In some ant colonies **there** *are* two or more queens.

All of the millions of ant colonies *have* a distinct smell.

Both **ants** and **termites** *have developed* complex social structures.

Have **you** ever *heard* about army ants?

Stay out of the path of the army **ants** in South America.

A worker **ant** *can leave* a scent trail for other ants in the colony.

There *are* literally **billions** of ants on this earth.

How many kinds of ants *have* **you** *seen*?

Ant's **jaws**, or mandibles, *open* and *shut* like a pair of pliers and can bite hard.

The **abdomen** of the ant *contains* not just one but two stomachs.

The only real job of the **queen** *is* egg production.

FINISH

Ants *can feel* but also *can smell* with their antennae.

Some **ants** can *spray* formic acid and kill other insects with it.

Most species of **ants** *live* two months or even less.

Each of the ant workers *can carry* 20 times its weight.

There *are* more than ten thousand **species** of ants.

Some of the red varieties of ants *can sting*.

Unit XIII: Object Complements–Direct and Indirect Objects

> For direct objects just say "what?" after the verb. Bingo! There they are.

> Hmmm.... What does that give you in that last sentence of yours?

Focus

The exercises in this unit give students practice finding direct and indirect objects.

Grammar Tips

★ As the first bird's final sentence illustrates, many sentences do not contain a direct object, and to be successful, students need to understand that direct objects must be nouns or pronouns, not adverbs, and must not be confused with the object of a preposition.

★ This unit deals exclusively with object complements, words that receive or complete (thus the name *complement*) the action of action verbs. The next unit takes up subject complements, which go with linking (state of being) verbs.

Teaching Tips

Begin a study of direct objects by writing two sentences on the board, one with an action verb and one with a linking verb, like *I phoned the teacher* and *I am a teacher*. Then ask which words in the sentences the word *teacher* is related to. In the first case, students easily see that *teacher* is receiving the action of the verb *phoned*, while in the second, it is essentially the same thing as the subject *I*.

Explain that direct objects answer the question *what?* or *whom?* stated immediately after the action verb. They do not answer *where?* or *when?* as in this sentence: *I phoned yesterday.* (*Yesterday* is an adverb.)

When students have a firm grasp of direct objects, introduce indirect objects, and point out that there will not be an indirect object unless there is already a direct object. Have them rule out all words in prepositional phrases, illustrating the difference with two sentences like *He gave **me** the assignment* (indirect object) and *He gave the assignment **to me*** (object of preposition).

The first exercise in this unit concentrates on direct objects while the second exercise and the maze require students to find both direct and indirect objects.

Parts of Speech Made Fun • Scholastic Teaching Resources

Name_____ Date _____

An Aardvark?

When the Dutch went to South Africa they saw an animal that they called an aardvark or "earth-pig." Do you know, or can you guess, what sort of an animal an aardvark really is?

Directions: To check your answer, circle the direct objects in the sentences below. (Your teacher may ask you to find the subjects and verbs first.) *Hint:* In two sentences there are no direct objects. Circle [none] at the end of those sentences. Then fit the direct objects (or the word *none*) into the grid. When you have entered all the correct words, using every answer space, the vertical column of boxes will spell out what sort of animal an aardvark is. An example has been done for you.

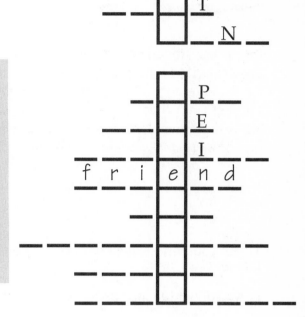

1. The news article mentioned a (friend) of mine. [none]

2. They are building a huge boat in their back yard. [none]

3. Tanya layered the cakes very carefully. [none]

4. Did you make that beautiful sculpture? [none]

5. Are you really going to Brazil over the winter break? [none]

6. Invite everyone in the class to the picnic. [none]

7. Are you planning more parties this summer? [none]

8. We put tape across the top and bottom of the poster. [none]

9. In that crazy outfit he is surely asking for trouble. [none]

10. She donated her old car to the charity auction. [none]

Parts of Speech Made Fun • Scholastic Teaching Resources

51

Direct and indirect objects

Name_____ Date _____

Hidden Scrambled Words

There is a message hidden in this exercise, but you will have to unscramble the letters that make it up in order to read it.

Directions: Underline and label all of the direct objects (*d.o.*) and indirect objects (*i.o.*) in the sentences below. Circle the first letter of each underlined word. Then unscramble the circled letters by fitting them into the blank spaces. The letters in sentences 1–4 make up the first two words; the letters in 5–8 make up the next three words; the letters in 9–12 make up the final word. **Hint:** Two sentences have no direct or indirect objects at all, and one of them has a direct but no indirect object. Also, some objects are compounds.

_ _O_ _ _ _ _N_ _ _L_ _ _F_ _H_ _ _B_ _ _ _ _ _ .

1. Did you send Nancy flowers for her birthday?

2. My music teacher assigned us opera and yodeling as projects.

3. Please pass the dessert to your brother.

4. Grandma gave us an electric organ for Christmas.

5. Lin promised Lou and Fred a tank of gas for driving her to school.

6. Did Mr. Choi leave her any of his vacation phone numbers?

7. Tomorrow we are going to the new bat exhibit at the zoo.

8. Aunt Pia is sending everyone lemons and oranges from Florida.

9. On the bus, Mandy told Bola a long story about her strange aunt.

10. Why are you looking in the refrigerator for the house keys?

11. The strong wind should give one of us a chance for an easy win.

12. In the first hand Andy dealt each of us a ten and a jack.

Name_____ Date _____

Maze

Directions: Find your way from the start to the finish by passing through 15 spaces that contain sentences in which the direct and indirect objects have been correctly identified. Direct objects are in **boldface**; indirect objects are in **boldface italics**. If the word is incorrectly identified, that area acts as a block and you must find another path. This maze also has areas with numbers and instructions. When you reach them, you will have to make choices, which may lead to false paths.

★ **Bonus:** How many correct spaces are there in the entire maze? _____

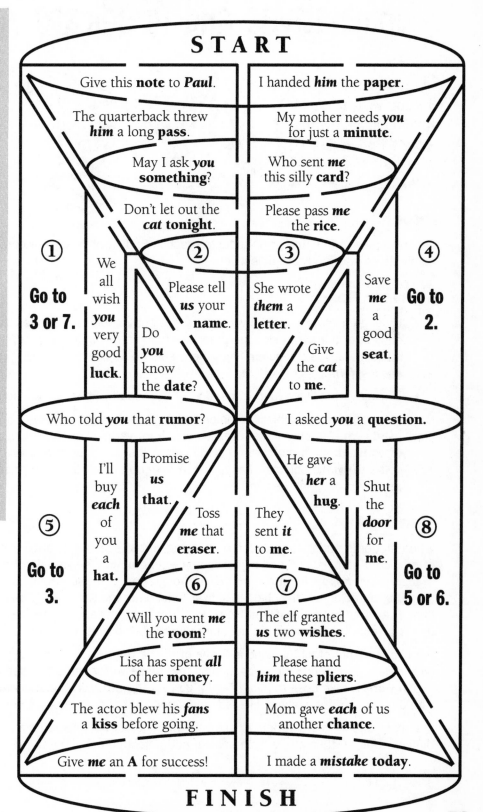

START

Give this **note** to *Paul*.

I handed *him* the **paper**.

The quarterback threw *him* a long **pass**.

My mother needs *you* for just a **minute**.

May I ask *you* **something**?

Who sent *me* this silly **card**?

Don't let out the *cat* tonight.

Please pass *me* the **rice**.

① Go to 3 or 7.

We all wish *you* very good **luck**.

② Please tell *us* your **name**.

③ She wrote *them* a **letter**.

Save *me* a good **seat**.

④ Go to 2.

Do *you* know the **date**?

Give the *cat* to me.

Who told *you* that **rumor**?

I asked *you* a **question**.

I'll buy *each* of you a **hat**.

Promise *us* that.

He gave *her* a **hug**.

Shut the **door** for me.

⑤ Go to 3.

Toss *me* that **eraser**.

They sent *it* to me.

⑧ Go to 5 or 6.

⑥ ⑦

Will you rent *me* the **room**?

The elf granted *us* two **wishes**.

Lisa has spent *all* of her **money**.

Please hand *him* these **pliers**.

The actor blew his *fans* a **kiss** before going.

Mom gave *each* of us another **chance**.

Give *me* an **A** for success!

I made a *mistake* today.

FINISH

Unit XIV: Subject Complements-Predicate Nominatives and Predicate Adjectives

I feel happy that the verb *to be* is the only linking verb that I need to look for.

Like most of your ideas, that one sounds silly to me.

Focus

The exercises in this unit give students practice finding both subject complements—predicate nominatives and predicate adjectives.

Grammar Tips

★ Linking (or state of being) verbs take subject complements, ones that refer back to the subject of the sentence. The predicate nominative is, in essence, the same thing as the subject—*She is a **teacher***—and the predicate adjective modifies the subject (*She is **successful***).

★ Linking verbs, like action verbs, do not necessarily have complements—*She is in the play*.

★ Most of the time subject complements are used with the verb *to be*, our most commonly used verb. But students must also watch for verbs like *feel, sound, taste,* and *smell* that are often used, as in the cartoon, as linking verbs, although they can also be used as action verbs that take objects—*Feel this soft material*. Other frequently used linking verbs are *seem, appear,* and *become*.

Teaching Tips

When students understand action and linking verbs (see Unit V, page 20), you can begin the study of predicate nominatives and adjectives by writing a simple example of each on the board: *I am a **teacher**; I am **happy***. Point out that even though one of these emphasized words is a noun and the other an adjective, they have a similar function in the sentence. Ask if students can see what it is. They may notice that both refer to *I*, the subject, and some may even see that, like direct objects, both answer the question *What?* stated after the verb.

Remind students of all the various forms of the verb *to be*—*am, is, are, was, were, have been, should have been,* and so on—cautioning that these words are also used as auxiliaries before action verbs—*have been running*. Finally, go over the other linking verbs mentioned above, ending with the verbs of the senses, like *feel* and *smell,* that can be used as both action and linking verbs.

The exercises in this unit deal exclusively with subject complements and grow increasingly difficult. Unit XV then mixes both subject and object complements.

Parts of Speech Made Fun • Scholastic Teaching Resources

Predicate nominatives and predicate adjectives

Name_____ Date _____

Word Find

All the subject complements in these sentences are hidden in the word find.

Directions: Identify all the subject complements (predicate nominatives and predicate adjectives) in the sentences below. (Your teacher may ask you to find the verbs and subjects first and to label the type of complement that each is—p.a. or p.n.) Then circle the answers hidden in the word find. The words run up, down, left, right, and diagonally in all four directions.
Hint: Two of the sentences have no subject complements and two have compound subject complements.

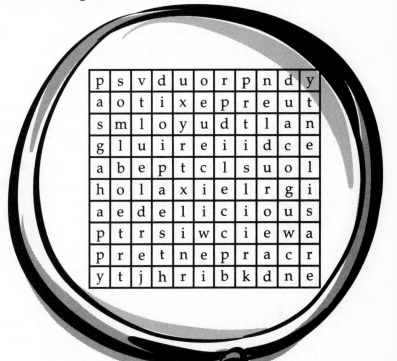

p	s	v	d	u	o	r	p	n	d	y
a	o	t	i	x	e	p	r	e	u	t
s	m	l	o	y	u	d	t	l	a	n
g	l	u	i	r	e	i	i	d	c	e
a	b	e	p	t	c	l	s	u	o	l
h	o	l	a	x	i	e	l	r	g	i
a	e	d	e	l	i	c	i	o	u	s
p	t	r	s	i	w	c	i	e	w	a
p	r	e	t	n	e	p	r	a	c	r
y	t	j	h	r	i	b	k	d	n	e

1. My gerbils are very happy in their large new cage.

2. After retirement, my father became a guide at the museum.

3. This black raspberry ice cream tastes delicious.

4. Why is Carmen in that tree?

5. You must have felt very proud and excited after your concert.

6. My uncle has been a carpenter all of his life.

7. Be absolutely silent!

8. His favorite colors were yellow and purple.

9. I have been at the mall all day long.

10. The owner of that rusty old car is, strangely, a rich politician.

Challenging predicate nominatives and predicate adjectives

Name_____ **Date** _____

64 Points

Earn points by finding and identifying subject complements—both predicate nominatives and predicate adjectives. Can you make the maximum number of points, 64?

Directions: Most, but not all, of the sentences below contain subject complements. Identify them by writing p.n. (predicate nominative) or p.a. (predicate adjective) over them. (Your teacher may ask you to find the subjects and verbs first.) You get 4 points for each correctly identified predicate nominative, 3 points for a correctly identified predicate adjective, and 5 points if you see that the sentence has no subject complement. Enter your score at the end of each sentence, then add up your sentence scores to see how close you came to the maximum of 64 points. **Hint:** If a sentence has a compound subject complement, you get points for each part that you identify.

Examples:
                           p.n.
           a. This is a new car. _4_
           b. We have been here before. _5_
(a. 4 points for *car*, a predicate nominative; b. 5 for no complement.)

1. The house across the street from me is a log cabin. ___

2. That tortilla smells too strong and spicy for me. ___

3. What are the sizes of your shoes and socks? ___

4. After the operation she seemed so weak and listless. ___

5. Has anyone here been to the new ice cream store? ___

6. Charlene has been a nurse, a doctor, and a therapist. ___

7. The road had become a sheet of ice in the winter storm. ___

8. Your gloves are on the shelf under the hall window. ___

9. Does this song sound appropriate for a solemn occasion? ___

10. Throughout the drill, the students remained calm and quiet. ___

11. Have there been any calls for me this evening? ___

12. That choice would have been a big mistake. ___

Parts of Speech Made Fun • Scholastic Teaching Resources

Review

Name _____

Date _____

Maze

Directions: Find your way from the start to the finish by passing through 31 areas in which subject complements have been correctly indicated. Predicate adjectives are in *italics* and predicate nominatives are in **boldface**. If the word is not a subject complement or is identified incorrectly, that area is a block and you must find another path.

Notice that to get from the bow half of the ship to the stern half, you must "leap" from "Go to 1" or "Go to 2."

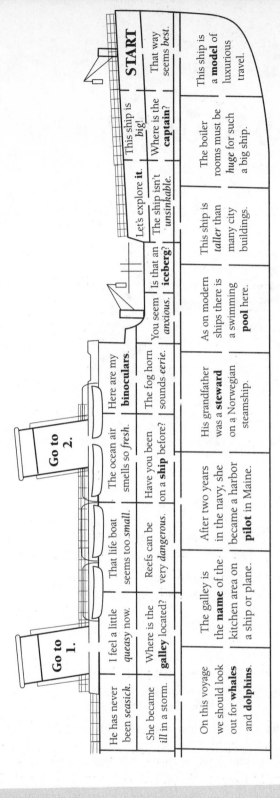

START

This ship is *big*!

Where is the **captain**?

That way seems *best*.

This ship is a **model** of luxurious travel.

Let's explore *it*.

The ship isn't *unsinkable*.

The boiler rooms must be *huge* for such a big ship.

Is that an **iceberg**?

This ship is *taller* than many city buildings.

You seem *anxious*.

As on modern ships there is a swimming **pool** here.

Here are my **binoculars**.

The fog horn sounds *eerie*.

His grandfather was a **steward** on a Norwegian steamship.

The ocean air smells so *fresh*.

Have you been on a **ship** before?

After two years in the navy, she became a harbor **pilot** in Maine.

Go to 2.

That life boat seems too *small*.

Reefs can be very *dangerous*.

The galley is the **name** of the kitchen area on a ship or plane.

I feel a little *queasy* now.

Where is the **galley** located?

On this voyage we should look out for **whales** and **dolphins**.

Go to 1.

He has never been *seasick*.

She became *ill* in a storm.

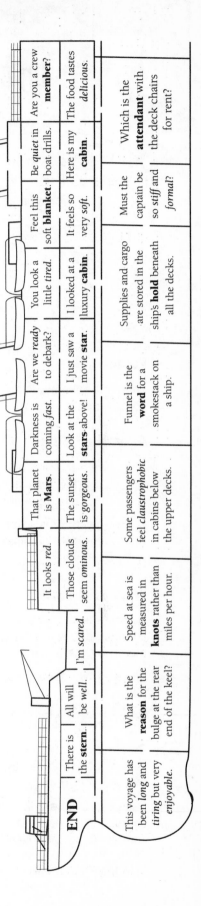

R.M.S. TITANIC

Are you a crew **member**?

Be *quiet* in boat drills.

Here is my **cabin**.

The food tastes *delicious*.

Which is the **attendant** with the deck chairs for rent?

Feel this soft **blanket**.

It feels so very *soft*.

Must the captain be so *stiff* and *formal*?

You look a little *tired*.

I looked at a luxury **cabin**.

Supplies and cargo are stored in the ship's **hold** beneath all the decks.

Are we *ready* to debark?

I just saw a movie **star**.

Funnel is the **word** for a smokestack on a ship.

2

Darkness is coming *fast*.

Look at the **stars** above!

Some passengers feel *claustrophobic* in cabins below the upper decks.

1

That planet is **Mars**.

The sunset is *gorgeous*.

Speed at sea is measured in **knots** rather than miles per hour.

It looks *red*.

Those clouds seem *ominous*.

What is the **reason** for the bulge at the rear end of the keel?

I'm *scared*.

All will be *well*.

This voyage has been *long* and tiring but very *enjoyable*.

END

There is the **stern**.

57

Unit XV: Mixed Complements

Action verbs can't be linking verbs, and vice versa.

Sound the alarms! That idea sounds even sillier than your others.

Focus

This unit asks students to find and distinguish between object complements and subject complements.

Grammar Tips

★ While the first bird is wrong, as the second bird quickly demonstrates, he is right about all but a few English verbs. The great majority of our verbs are action verbs that, when transitive, take object complements—direct and, occasionally, indirect objects.

★ Object complements do not appear more frequently, however, than subject complements (predicate nominatives and adjectives) since the linking verb *to be* is our most frequently used verb.

Teaching Tips

Before asking students to deal with mixed complements, teach them to check whether the complement is the same thing as the subject or is modifying the subject. If it's the same or is modifying the subject, it is a subject complement; if neither is the case, it's an object.

Write up two sentences, one with a predicate nominative and one with a direct object —*That animal is a dog*; *That animal has fleas*—and point out that in the first case, the predicate nominative *dog* is the same thing as the subject *animal*. In the second sentence, however, the direct object *fleas* is not at all the same thing as the subject.

Before giving students the exercises in this unit, you might want to remind them that they should beware of sentences that contain no complements at all—*That dog is scratching*; *He is sitting very close to your dog*.

Each exercise is a little more difficult than the one before it. Some of the sentences contain no complements at all to emphasize the fact that often our verbs are followed only by modifiers, not complements. Although the directions make it optional for students to identify subjects and verbs in the sentences before looking for complements, it is advisable to require them to do so and also have them eliminate prepositional phrases before identifying the subjects and verbs.

Parts of Speech Made Fun • Scholastic Teaching Resources

Name _____ **Date** _____

A Punny Reply

Rosemary and her friend Lily were gossiping.

"Did you hear about Violet?" whispered Lily.

"No, what now?" asked Rosemary.

"She took one of her mother's lipsticks and is strutting around with lipstick smeared all over her mouth," replied Lily.

"Oh, no. What color is it?" Rosemary asked.

Lily thought for a moment, then laughed and said: "____ ____ ___ ____."

Directions: To reveal Lily's reply, underline and label all the complements (*d.o.*—direct object, *i.o.*—indirect object, *p.n.*—predicate nominative, *p.a.*—predicate adjective) in the sentences on page 60. (Your teacher may ask you to find the subjects and verbs first.) Then write the letter in parentheses on the line with the matching number **in the section that corresponds to the type of complement** that you have found. An example has been done for you. *Hint:* In some sentences there are compound complements and in one sentence there is no complement at all.

Direct Object	Predicate Adjective	Indirect Object	Predicate Nominative
__ __ __ __ *e* __ ' __ 1 2 3 4 5 6 7	__ __ __ __ __ __ 1 2 3 4 5 6	__ __ __ 1 2 3	__ __ __ __ 1 2 3 4

Name _____ **Date** _____

A Punny Reply (continued)

                                        d.o.
1. This year **(3a)** the farmers **(1r)** planted their crops **(5e)** early.

2. My friend Al **(2g)** is a freshman **(3s)** at Lincoln High School **(4i)**.

3. This birthday cake **(1t)** tastes old **(3l)** and stale **(6s)**.

4. The dryer **(4n)** has eaten your shirt **(2i)** and one **(7d)** sock **(4l)**.

5. My father **(5t)** gave me **(3e)** a hug **(7s)** after the track meet **(4p)**.

6. We poured the milk **(6t)** into the chocolate **(1r)** sauce **(2w)**

7. After the game **(5o)** we sat on the stairs **(3c)** and waited for my dad **(2u)**.

8. Despite the blizzard **(4y)**, the cottage **(6e)** was warm **(4i)** and cozy **(1t)**.

9. Save us **(1a)** some seats **(3o)** at the front **(2g)** of the auditorium **(5s)**.

10. The desert **(3k)** had once **(5l)** been an ocean **(4e)** and also a rich valley **(2o)**.

11. The shopkeeper **(7y)** paid Sari **(2r)** ten dollars **(1v)** for her old doll **(3t)**.

12. Their new **(2m)** car is already rusty **(5p)**.

13. Are you **(1m)** very **(4n)** sure **(2u)** about that answer **(3i)**?

14. The general **(1r)** became a television **(3c)** commentator **(1r)** after the war **(5s)**.

Parts of Speech Made Fun • Scholastic Teaching Resources

Name _____ **Date** _____

Guaranteed Groaner

Question: **What's the difference between a fish and a piano?**

Directions: To answer this silly riddle, underline and label all the complements (*d.o.*—direct object, *i.o.*—indirect object, *p.n.*—predicate nominative, *p.a.*—predicate adjective) in the sentences below. (Your teacher may ask you to find the subjects and verbs first.) Then write the word in the appropriate space in the answer grid in the section that corresponds to the type of complement that you have identified. The riddle's answer will appear in the column of vertical boxes. An example has been done for you.

Hint: Some sentences have compound complements and two sentences have no complements at all. Also, be sure not to leave empty spaces.

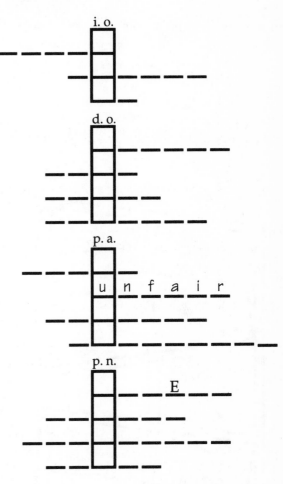

i. o.

d. o.

p. a.

u n f a i r

p. n.

E

1. The driving test seemed quite unfair to the
   nervous teenager. *(p.a. over "unfair")*

2. What did Tina give Roland for Valentine's Day?

3. Abraham Lincoln became the president on
   March 4, 1861.

4. High in the tree was a huge eagle's nest with two chicks in it.

5. Willie, our scrambling quarterback, threw Denny a long lateral.

6. He was my best friend but also my biggest critic.

7. There were boxes and boxes of old letters in his attic.

8. To the jury his testimony seemed completely sincere.

9. For the huge dessert Janice used three pints of whipping cream.

10. Will Gregory be an usher at Leif's wedding?

11. The liberal teacher gave us another chance.

12. The smoke from the fire smelled sooty and dangerous.

Mixed Complements

Name_____ **Date** _____

Double Maze

Directions: This is a double maze. One path leads through sentences that have only subject complements—predicate nominatives and predicate adjectives. The other leads through sentences that have only object complements—direct and a few indirect objects. On the subject complement path, you may pass only through areas containing sentences with subject complements; areas with object complements act as blocks. On the object complement path, the rule is reversed and subject complements act as blocks. **Hint:** There are a few false paths to make a difficult maze even more difficult. The correct paths go through 23 subject complement areas and 24 object complement areas.

START

Has Paula been happy with her new car?

Somebody here must have a pencil or a pen.

You must be a very patient worker today.

We have a hard journey ahead of us.

After school we can play chess.

Experience is an excellent teacher.

Please be very quiet.

I sent both of them cards for their birthdays.

Call me in the morning and wake me up.

Most people like cats.

Give him this rag and tell him to use it.

Have you ever seen a three-toed sloth?

Luis must have been so happy from that news.

Rosalinda is planning a big birthday bash.

You seem very sad and upset this evening.

Little Susan looked cute in her lilac suit.

Did Mika give you those good concert tickets?

Hang your coat here.

Are you the manager?

This soup is much too salty for me.

He seemed more careful after his fall.

Who is your new history teacher?

Did they all believe that silly story?

After an hour Sarah finally found her ring.

The full moon looked huge this evening.

The president discussed his foreign policy.

The truth became a lie.

Which book did she assign you today?

Charlene wrote a story about her parakeet.

The car needs gas.

The lightning bolt struck our old silo.

Does your milk taste a little bit sour?

He has been a carpenter for three years.

My mail carrier has been sick for a month.

We should have a flashlight in the tent.

This morning the fog was very thick.

He felt sorry about being so thoughtless.

The cheese smells rotten.

We took turns as pitcher.

The hood of our old car has become rusty.

Are you the owner of this red scooter?

Cross the little bridge at the end of the path.

What did you tell them about the movie?

I can play many games on my new computer.

After the game the girls looked very upset.

Why is Joanne so far ahead of the rest of us?

He seems very anxious.

I have seen that cute dog once before.

Our cottage overlooks a tidal river.

Give us a hand!

That last note sounded a bit flat to me.

The journey was hard but rewarding.

FINISH SUBJECT COMPLEMENTS

FINISH OBJECT COMPLEMENTS

We've reached the end of a long road.

Do you feel sure about this path?

Answer Key

Unit I

Page 6: Finding Nouns: 1. vegetables, eggplant 2. roses, yard 3. Gary, oatmeal 4. order, dinner, waiter 5. Olivia, relative, king
Message: Very good work

Noun Find: 1. reader, reality 2. bride, banker 3. canoe, ice (extra word in grid, the verb *lain*) 4. party, canary 5. lamp, lane

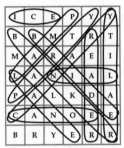

Page 7: 1. Henry, hippo, top, house 2. tiger, tear, tutu 3. price, plaster, Paris, Paul, porch, paste 4. sailors, sandwiches, soldiers 5. beauty, bag, Brenda, baby.
Hidden message: OK

Page 8: The correct path passes through: 1. Is the...noun? 2. Many dogs...*cats*. 3. My *friend*! 4. He's called *Nosy*. 5. Dachshunds...*badgers*. 6. Some dogs...*fur*. 7. They can...*pounds*. 8. good *muscles* 9. What is...*name*? 10. He...*kids*. 11. No *fleas*! 12. A *bone*! 13. Like a...*home*.
Bonus: 17, including *legs, hair, dachshund, and hounds.*

Unit II

Page 10: 1. Underlined Adjectives: 1. easy 2. muddy 3. low 4. lovely, yellow 5. new, Italian 6. pleasant 7. helpful, troublesome 8. mashed, full 9. tiny, portable 10. eager (Order in grid, top to bottom: easy, troublesome, full, mashed, Italian, lovely, eager, muddy, portable, tiny new, low, pleasant, helpful, yellow)
Message: You have done well.

Page 11: Adjectives: 1. a, small, the, the, old 2. The, only, the, orange 3. Every, these, a, short 4. dumb, summer 5. a, difficult, organ, a, short 6. All, those, easy 7. That, expensive, tasteless 8. Every these, successful, extraordinary. 9. an, overgrown, a, special, the, deep 10. Sad, any, that, ordinary.
First letters: a–8, d–3, e–5, o–6, s–7, t–11.

Page 12: The correct path passes through: 1. My boat...seats. 2. The skies...*clear*. 3. The roof...*steep*. 4. The *screen*...open. 5. Is Don...*sick*? 6. I love...*sweater*. 7. Is this...way? 8. Pass me...please. 9. I like...soup. 10. Your dog...*intelligent*. 11. My *hiking*...out. 12. She read...had. 13. It's an...car. 14. This milk...*sour*. 15. Are there...cookies? 16. Pat is...am. 17. I found...path.

Unit III

Page 14: Pronouns: 1. herself, this 2. everyone, me 3. all, you, yourselves, several 4. one 5. few, us, you, himself, her 6. most, themselves 7. that, she, herself 8. any, you 9. This, he, anyone
Answer: 24 (Don't forget Hawaii and Alaska.)

Page 15: Pronouns: 1. you, somebody, that (before looks) 2. one, that, I 3. anyone, this, one 4. Either, me, who, she, both, them 5. anyone, what 6. who 7. All, what
Message: You have circled twenty.

Page 16: The correct path passes through: 1. **This** is...book. 2. Does **everyone**...today? 3. Jennifer seems...**herself**. 4. **This** is easy. 5. **He** seems sad. 6. **Who** is...game? 7. Think about **me**. 8. He told...**himself**. 9. **That** is...joke. 10. I love **it**! 11. Tell **whoever**...you.! 12. Try **some** of these. 13. **Who** is...you? 14. **Each** of...team. 15. **That** seems...go. 16. **Many** of...play. 17. They praised **themselves**. 18. **Few** of...time. 19. May we...bar? 20. **You** call her. 21. Tai helped **us**. 22. Is **that**...tractor? 23. **Who** is leading? 24. **I am**...behind. 25. You should...want. 26. Pick just...them. 27. Which of...idea? 28. You can...**yourself**! 29. Has **everyone**...home? 30. **He** has gone. 31. Tell me...mean. 32. **Both** of...made. 33. **Someone** called us. 34. We told...**ourselves**. 35. **Many** of...well. 36. **We** enjoy soccer. 37. **Which** of...yours? 38. Did **anybody**...yet? 39. This is...fun.

Unit IV

Page 18: n = noun, pro = pronoun, adj = adjective 1. that–pro, cookie–n, that–adj 2. Which–adj, cookie–adj, cutter–n, those–adj, clay–adj 3. Which–pro, these–pro, clay–n, heavy–adj 4. paper–n, which–pro, porch–n, that–pro 5. either–pro, any–pro, those–adj, flavors–n 6. either–adj, one–pro, who–pro, nose–n 7. one–pro, homework–adj, assignments–n, some–adj, poems–n, that–pro 8. This–adj, homework–n, some–pro, that–pro, 9. hospital–n, ice–n, that–pro 10. Those–pro, who–pro, this–adj, candidate–n, all–adj, new–adj **Answer:** 206

Page 19: The correct path passes through: 1. n) Is that...crow? 2. a) **song** book 3. p) **That** is good. 4. n) A crow...**tree**. 5. p) Look at **this**! 6. a) His feathers...**dark**. 7. p) **Which** of...you? 8. n) Can he...**dark**? 9. a) **Most** birds fly. 10. n) Crows can...**tools**. 11. p) Are **some**...there? 12. p) It's a...know. 13. a) We can...path. 14. a) **this** one 15. n) a big **bird** 16. p) Try **all**...them. 17. p) **One** is cawing. 18. p) **What** do...mean? 19. n) Does it...**house**? 20. a) It has...ball! 21. n) Do you...**golf**? 22. p) **Who** won?

Unit V

Page 21: 1. fits 2. tested 3. drive 4. Draw 5. satisfied, appointed 6. requires 7. praised 8. trickles 9. brought 10. produces 11. crawled, hid
Answer: It is a watchdog.

Page 22: m = main verb; aux = auxiliary verb 1. will–aux, be–aux, giving–m 2. has–aux, been–aux, asked–m 3. do–aux, have–m 4. should–aux, have–aux, known–m, was–aux, going–m 5. Has–aux, been–aux, using–m 6. did–aux, reach–m, had–aux, been–m 7. had–aux, been–aux, looking–m, would–aux, have–aux, seen–m 8. Could–aux, have–aux, helped–m 9. have–aux, been–aux, doing–m 10. might–aux, have–aux, been–aux, asked–m
Hidden message: BIKE

Page 23: act = active verb aux = auxiliary verb, link = linking verb 1. has–aux, been–link 2. seems–link, can–aux, be–link 3. Have–aux, decided–act 4. searched–act, came–act 5. would– aux, have–aux, felt–link, had–aux, seen–act 6. lay–act, looked–link 7. Can–aux, do–act, gave–act 7. was–link, could–aux, have–aux, been–link
Message: They can not walk backwards.

Page 24: Action verb path: 1. I gave...yesterday. 2. Hold on tight! 3. Do they...store? 4. I love pears. 5. Think about it. 6. Vicky...foot. 7. They have...milk. 8. Do your...homework. 9. The magician.... 10. Was he helping? 11. Cross...here. 12. I forgot...book. 13. Feel this...satin. 14. Sound the alarm! 15. Try the...computer. 16. He was...soup. 17. The teacher...quiz. 18. We are...car. 19. I need...haircut. 20. I wished...luck. 21. Don't drive...fast. 22. I just...dollar. 23. Can you...it?
Bonus: 1. Do you have...pets? 2. Smell this mint. 3. I have had...cold. 4. Look at this!

Linking verb path: 1. You should...there! 2. The cake...done. 3. They seem...unhappy! 4. I have...sick. 5. You look tired. 6. I've been...once. 7. How old...you? 8. It is hot today. 9. He should...actor. 10. That smells good! 11. She looks pretty. 12. He has...quiet. 13. He was...careful. 14. My dad...angry. 15. His voice...fine. 16. It feels...soft! 17. Everyone... scared. 18. Is she...cold? 19. He seems...smart. 20. That hat...silly. 21. This tastes sour. 22. The trip...fun. 23. Here it is!
Bonus: 1. Are you sure? 2. Please be very still. 3. There has been a fire. 4. Has he been away?

Unit VI
Page 26: 1. happily, loudly, suddenly, speedily 2. Sadly, early 3. angrily, slowly, Unfortunately, immediately, completely 4. Usually, slowly, badly, really 5. truly, sympathetically, unhappily, absolutely 6. eventually, softly, quietly, patiently, creatively 7. supposedly, securely, totally, permanently
Hidden message: 150

Page 27: 1. so, enviously 2. again, today, unhappily, however, very 3. Happily, always, here, sympathetically 4. Sometimes, almost, Yesterday, loudly 5. Really, diplomatically, always 6. miserably, often, somewhat 7. certainly, not, angrily, now 8. tomorrow, hurriedly 9. then, sadly, very, Maybe.
Answer: 1931

Page 28: The correct path goes through: 1. These dresses...women. 2. I'll **happily**...hat. 3. I could...day. 4. This cone...delicious. 5. Do these...**well**? 6. **Here** is...cow. 7. Would you...those? 8. **Surely** you...one! 9. Don't knock...platter! 10. I'm feeling...early. 11. **Tomorrow** we...rose. 12. I'll buy...**later**. 13. That bat...much. 14. They also...here. 15. We're running...know. 16. This place...us.

Unit VII
Page 30: Prepositions: 1. across, from, of 2. From, around 3. For, about 4. to, with 5. Except, on, to 6. In, during, through, on 7. After, up 8. After, beyond 9. about, under, for, of 10. Against, out, along 11. through 12. of, from, into 13. of, off, over, towards 14. after, without, into, like
Answer: 1939

Page 31: prep = preposition, adv = adverb
1. before–prep, outside–prep, afterwards–adv 2. inside–adv, towards–prep 3. Underneath–prep, from–prep, behind–prep
4. Despite–prep, before–adv (bonus), still–adv
5. Throughout–prep, upwards–adv, around–prep
6. across–prep, around–adv (bonus), without–prep

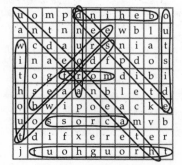

Page 32: The correct path goes through: 1. It's so early **for** a field trip! 2. He went **behind** a rock. 3. **Before** lunch I need to call home. 4. He jumped **over** that boulder easily. 5. Stand **behind** the rock. 6. He's walking **up** that cliff! 7. One **of** us should go. 8. His horns go **around** his head. 9. He's looking right **at** us. 10. Don't go **off** the path. 11. Stand **by** me. 12. **Beyond** that ram I think I see an antelope. 13. I think everything is fun **except** the wind. 14. It's too cold **for** me. 15. This is the end **of** a great day.

Unit VIII
Page 34: Conjunctions: 1. and 2. before, or, because, when 3. and, if 4. Since 5. Although, and 6. Until, than 7. and, yet
Answer: It was a clear day.

Page 35: Conjunctions: 1. and, if (after– preposition) 2. since, yet, than 3. because (before– preposition) 4. or, when 5. after, but, because 6. for (For– preposition) 7. As, and (after– preposition)
Answer: 3

Page 36: The path to the finish goes through: 1. He doesn't...anymore. 2. I haven't...born. 3. I'll hang...want it. 4. **When** Marty...book. 5. Oliver...over. 6. **While** you...kitchen. 7. **If** you...call me. 8. **After** you...trash. 9. It's much...thought! 10. Marcia...interests. 11. I don't...story. 12. **Although** I...away. 13. **As** I...winter. 14. **Because**...sick. 15. Carla **and**...band. 16. Be sure...leave. 17. We weren't...comfortable. 18. You get...about it. 19. **If** you...succeed. **Bonus:** 2 (1. I like fish...it. 2. I'll pick...is ready.)

Unit IX
Page 38: The correct path goes through: 1. Oh, no...easy. 2. Well, I.... 3. Wow!... 4. Now, now.... 5. Yes, indeed...well. 6. Great!.... 7. Hmm,.... 8. Bravo!.... 9. So, just... 10. Well, I've.... 11. Hey,.... 12. Darn, I'm... 13. Yo,.... 14. Oh, I.... 15. What!.... 16. Behold,.... 17. Boo!.... 18. Alas,.... 19. There!.... 20. Hooray!....
Bonus: 24 (1. Rats!...path. 2. Oh, dear, I feel...path. 3. My, what...had. 4. Goodness!)

Unit X
Page 40: adj = adjective, n = noun, pro = pronoun, v = verb
1. side–adj, left–v, that–pro, duck–n 2. right–adj, hand–n, duck–v 3. Hand–v, that–adj, note–n (no letter in grid), right–n. 4. that–pro, need–v (no letter in grid), rest–n, flat–adj, Watch–v, rest–adj. 5. Neither–pro, rest–v, all–pro, rest–n, those–adj
Answer: Short version: "Hello, Mary," says mellow Harry.

Page 41: The correct path goes through: 1. I think...**fast**. 2. **That** is...ice cream. 3. The **corner**...bread. 4. The house...huge. 5. **This** problem...quickly. 6. **Which** one...take? 7. I write...**this**. 8. He plays...do. 9. I think...way. 10. What do...**that**? 11. Did Cheryl...way? 12. He looked...happy. 13. Your **watch**...break. 14. I think...correct.

Unit XI
Page 43: s = simple subject, v = verb (simple predicate)
1. package–s; arrived–v 2. bird–s; flies–v 3. Dorothy–s; cleaned–v 4. friends–s; were having–v 5. dogs–s; were–v 6. uncle–s; has been–v 7. fellow–s; laughed–v 8. sailboat–s; can win–v

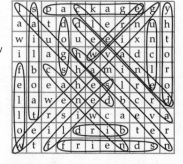